# LITERACY
# ENGAGEMENT
THROUGH
PERITEXTUAL
ANALYSIS

PUBLISHED IN PARTNERSHIP WITH
**National Council of Teachers of English**

# LITERACY ENGAGEMENT
## THROUGH PERITEXTUAL ANALYSIS

*edited by*
SHELBIE WITTE,
DON LATHAM,
*and* MELISSA GROSS

ALA
Editions
CHICAGO / 2019

ISBN: 978-0-8389-1768-8 (paper)

**Library of Congress Cataloging-in-Publication Data**

Names: Witte, Shelbie, editor. | Latham, Don, 1959- editor. | Gross, Melissa, editor.
Title: Literacy engagement through peritextual analysis / edited by Shelbie Witte, Don Latham, and Melissa Gross.
Description: Chicago : ALA Editions, 2019. | Includes index.
Identifiers: LCCN 2018030426 | ISBN 9780838917688 (print : alk. paper)
Subjects: LCSH: Paratext. | Critical thinking—Study and teaching. | Information literacy—Study and teaching. | Media literacy—Study and teaching.
Classification: LCC Z242.P37 L57 2018 | DDC 370.15/2—dc23 LC record available at https://lccn.loc.gov/2018030426

Cover design by Alejandra Diaz. Composition by Kim Thornton in the Chaparral Pro and Museo typefaces.

♾ This paper meets the requirements of ANSI/NISO Z39.48–1992 (Permanence of Paper).

Printed in the United States of America

23 22 21 20 19      5 4 3 2 1

# CONTENTS

# FOREWORD

**AS A CHILD, A TEENAGER, AND A LONG-TIME ADULT, I HAVE ALWAYS STARED** at book covers, tried to figure out why an author's birthplace may influence what gets noticed (or not) between the covers of a given text, and read a chapter's source notes as preliminary scaffolds for what eventually unfolded in the chapter. And, surprise, surprise, I never considered such behaviors eccentric or geeklike. If anything, I imagined myself a sleuth getting closer and closer to solving some unidentified mystery.

The fact that similar actions were rarely voiced or done by students during my grade school teaching days or later while teaching at the college level was disappointing. In hindsight, what I would have given for a copy of *Literacy Engagement through Peritextual Analysis!* First, this book's logical and timely four-part structure speaks to the need for a theoretically grounded pedagogy that focuses on literary, informational, and digital texts at a time when fake news and unqualified claims often go unharnessed.

A second measure of this book's timeliness is its attention to visual literacy and the peritextual analysis of nonprint texts. Without explicit instruction in these vitally important areas, the youth of today stand little chance of successfully navigating the communication networks that are forming on all sides and at varying levels—the very networks that a status quo curriculum is ill-equipped to decode and reconceptualize.

Finally, thanks to the multidisciplinary backgrounds of this volume's editors and chapter authors, *Literacy Engagement through Peritextual Analysis* is unequalled in its approach to engaging literate actions using peritextual analysis. Authentic materials, examples of lesson plans and units, and critical literacy strategies honed to perfection virtually beg to be implemented. Full disclosure: reading this edited collection in preparing to write the foreword took me longer than anticipated because I could not resist taking marginal notes and then converting them into minilessons for use in my literacy teacher education courses this coming semester.

Donna Alvermann
The University of Georgia
May 12, 2018

# ACKNOWLEDGMENTS

**WE WOULD LIKE TO THANK THE ALAN FOUNDATION (WWW.ALAN-YA.ORG) FOR** awarding a grant to support the foundational study of these ideas.

# INTRODUCTION— MORE THAN WHITE NOISE

## Mining the Peritext for Literacy Engagement

SHELBIE WITTE

MALIK WAS A STUDENT IN MY EIGHTH-GRADE ENGLISH LANGUAGE ARTS class in 2006. As the class entered to begin the day, Malik strolled over to see what I was unpacking from the just-arrived box of young adult fiction and nonfiction books for my classroom library. "Are we gonna be reading this?" he asked, picking up a copy of the graphic novel *Deogratias: A Tale of Rwanda.*[1] I explained that if it was a book he chose to read, then he was welcome to check out a copy. Without a word, Malik picked up the book again, signed his name on the checkout list, and sat down to read.

Later that period, during my one-on-one reading workshop check-ins with students, I asked Malik what he had learned so far about Rwanda. The book, a vividly powerful fictional account of the Rwandan genocide, could be intense and rightfully disturbing. "I'm still pretty confused about what's happening," he admitted. I asked Malik what he learned from the historical overview in the preface or if he could make inferences from the book jacket. "Nah, that's just some white noise. . . . I always jump straight in to read the real stuff." Malik had avoided the peritext and had missed the opportunity to have the historical scaffolding needed to better understand the events of the story.

Malik's characterization of any supplemental parts of a book as "white noise," meaningless commotion or chatter, has stayed with me as I've considered and written about the ways in which adolescents engage with the books and media that surround them. Clearly, these elements are not meaningless, and yet, many of our students avoid reading them. Although Malik's dismissal of the peritext is nothing new to classroom teachers and librarians who want our students to engage with the complete text, we have long needed a way to pedagogically approach peritext in a more substantial way. How can we help our students understand the purpose and function of peritext? How can we use peritext to support critical thinking and evaluation of information?

The Peritextual Literacy Framework gives clarity to the white noise Malik describes. Melissa Gross and Don Latham drew upon Gérard Genette's foundational definition to provide an approach to peritext applicable to print and nonprint texts.[2] Using the Peritextual Literacy Framework as a teaching and thinking tool allows teachers and librarians the opportunity to guide students in focusing on the important functions of peritextual elements and recognizing their purpose in informing and supporting the text proper. Although the idea of peritext is not new, the Peritextual Literacy Framework is a groundbreaking approach to providing a common vocabulary and guidepost for teachers and librarians and, ultimately, all readers. Some functions of peritext (a glossary, for example) support the reader in understanding the text, while other functions (author's note, resource lists) enrich or enhance the reader's experience. This built-in differentiation has often been overlooked in pedagogical terms and provides a multitude of opportunities. This collection brings together a talented group of educators and librarians, each taking up the work of peritext in different ways. Each of the contributors uses a variety of texts and grade levels to explore peritext's function in the further understanding of the text.

The collection begins with Melissa Gross's foundational work of peritext and the Peritextual Literacy Framework, providing an overview of each as an anchor for the work shared in the collection. Illustrating the full use of the Peritextual Literacy Framework, Don Latham presents a case study of the use of young adult nonfiction, taking advantage of all the peritextual elements as an introduction to using peritext in the classroom.

The next section of the collection explores the ways in which we can use peritextual analysis to strengthen students' visual literacy skills. Crag Hill works with a high school English classroom to critically compare and contrast the function of two graphic novel covers. Librarian Jill Slay shares how she supports her high school's reading initiative by matching students to books using book cover speed dating, allowing students to make inferences about a book's potential match with their interests. Sean Connors and Erin Daugherty focus on the promotional function of peritext, exploring the ways in which the covers on young adult fiction interface between the text and its potential audience. And Katie Rybakova shares how college students in an Introduction to Literature course use Socratic Circles to discuss existentialist themes represented through the peritextual analysis of canonical book covers.

The third section of the collection focuses on using peritextual analysis to strengthen students' critical thinking. Rebecca Weber and Kevin Dyke explore using the author's note in young adult historical fiction to investigate primary sources related to the 1921 Tulsa Race Riot. Luciana de Oliveira, Loren Jones, and Sharon Smith investigate dust jackets with first-grade students, providing opportunities for classroom discourse and critical thinking in developing readers. Pushing the boundaries of peritext, Antero Garcia and Bud Hunt examine the ways in which *Cathy's Book* challenges the notion of the physical boundaries of a book, critiquing not only where but how readers connect with the text.

A collection on peritextual analysis of text would not be complete without an examination of how the functions of peritext and the Peritextual Literacy Framework exist within nonprint texts. Hyerin Bak and Josey McDaniel present a case study of high school students' peritextual analysis of online news articles. From a media literacy perspective, Peter Kunze examines the peritextual elements and the implications of the packaging of Disney films. And in a culmination of popular culture texts, Jennifer Dail, Kyle Jones, and Glenn Chance provide opportunities for students to analyze the peritext of a documentary film about graffiti artist Banksy, applying the knowledge in their own text creations.

We hope this collection invites you to consider, or reconsider, the ways in which peritextual analysis can enhance students' engagement with the full text, as authors intended it. We hope that the ideas put forward here help you visualize ways of implementing the Peritextual Literacy Framework with a variety of texts in your classrooms and libraries. And most important, we hope that you will find ways to help students think more critically about the texts that they read, see, and hear.

## NOTES

1. Jean-Phillipe Stassen, *Deogratias: A Tale of Rwanda* (New York: First Second, 2006).

2. Melissa Gross and Don Latham, "The Peritextual Literacy Framework: Using the Functions of Peritext to Support Critical Thinking," *Library and Information Science Research* 39, no. 2 (2017): 116–23.

# PART I

# AN OVERVIEW OF PERITEXTUAL ANALYSIS

*We should make a dance called the Peritext!*

—One student to another

(1)

# Grounding Our Work Theoretically

## *The Peritextual Literacy Framework*

### MELISSA GROSS

**IN EARLY 2016, WITH THE HELP OF AN ASSEMBLY ON LITERATURE FOR ADO-**
lescents of the National Council of Teachers of English (ALAN) Foundation
grant, an after-school peritext book club met once a month for five months to
begin testing the newly developed Peritextual Literacy Framework (PLF).[1] The
PLF (see the appendix) provides a scaffold for the comprehension of media,
assisting the reader or user in deciding to engage with a work, in evaluating the
content of the work, and in understanding the nature of the work by analyzing
its peritextual elements.

Peritext is the elements of a work that surround the main content and help
to mediate between the work and its readers. Examples of common peritext
often provided in books include the title page, table of contents, index, and
source notes. The analysis of peritext can increase comprehension of a work
and assist in the development of critical thinking and information literacy;
however, little has been written about methods of embedding peritext into
information literacy instruction. The peritext book club, which is the source of
the quotation that opens this chapter and which is described more fully later in
the chapter, was a resounding success. It demonstrated that the middle school
participants enjoyed learning about peritext, the terminology used in the PLF,

and how peritext functions to deepen understanding of a work. This chapter introduces the PLF and explains its theoretical base.

## The Theory of Paratext

Paratext is a concept that was developed by Gérard Genette.[2] He used this term to describe elements that are part of a work (peritext) and elements outside a work (epitext) that influence perceptions of the work and mediate a reader's engagement with a work. In developing his theory of paratext, Genette mainly discussed books, and, as previously noted, examples of peritextual elements in books include the title page, table of contents, index, and source notes among others (see the appendix). Epitext is not part of the book but, rather, points to it. Examples of epitext include book reviews, author websites, and works of critical literary analysis. Genette defines paratext in this way: paratext = peritext + epitext. The PLF focuses solely on peritext, filling a gap in Genette's theory by identifying the functions of peritext and placing peritextual elements into logical categories.

Genette was interested in analyzing the paratext associated with printed books and noted that though all books have paratext, they do not consistently provide the same kinds of paratext. For example, not all books include a foreword, glossary, bibliography, and the like, which means that paratextual analysis needs to assess individual works and that both the presence and the absence of paratext can be the focus of a paratextual analysis. For Genette,

> defining a paratextual element consists of determining its location (the question *where?*); the date of its appearance and, if need be, its disappearance (*when?*); its mode of existence, verbal or other (*how?*); the characteristics of its situation of communication—its sender and addressee (*from whom? to whom?*); and the functions that its message aims to fulfill (*to do what?*).[3]

Paratext has been widely adopted in the study of narrative and literary analysis.[4] It has been studied in a variety of disciplines to investigate not only the book but also a diversity of media, including fan fiction, film, DVDs, digital texts, networked media, and transmedia.[5] There have also been several studies of the paratext provided in children's books. These studies are interested in paratext and emergent literacy, the development of reading skills, and how paratext promotes interactivity between texts and readers. A primary focus has been on picture books and how paratext supports comprehension and appreciation and enriches the reading experience.[6] However, authors also observe that although there are many potential benefits (including media literacy) that can come from the examination of paratext, insufficient attention has been paid to it in educational environments.[7]

## The Peritextual Literacy Framework

Although much has been written about paratext, and specifically about peritext, Gross and Latham were the first to describe peritext as a kind of literacy.[8] However, even though the PLF has relevance across a range of media types for both their use and production, peritextual literacy is not conceptualized as a framework that subsumes other literacies. Rather, it promotes a skill that has significance for a variety of other literacies, such as information literacy, media literacy, digital literacy, visual literacy, cyber literacy, and information fluency. The PLF also offers skills that are relevant for transliteracy—"the ability to competently read, write, and interact across a range of platforms"—as well as basic skills such as reading and writing.[9]

As noted, the PLF concentrates on the functions of peritext and does not examine the role of epitext in relation to works. The PLF categorizes the functions of peritext into six types: production, promotional, navigational, intratextual, supplemental, and documentary. The PLF identifies each of the types of peritext, provides examples of the kind of peritextual elements that support the function, and provides questions to consider when assessing particular peritextual functions. The example elements are not exhaustive but, rather, suggestive and are largely taken from printed books. Many of these elements are also used in other kinds of media, and other kinds of media may provide additional peritextual elements that support the functions of peritext. The analysis of peritextual elements across a variety of media provides an ongoing opportunity for research.

*Production.* The job of production elements is to uniquely identify a work. These elements, such as the author's name, copyright, and ISBN information, establish what work the reader has in hand, or wishes to locate, differentiating it from other works and providing information about the work's creation. These elements allow the reader to refer to and locate works as well as to make comparisons between works. Understanding production elements, where they appear in a work, and how they can be used makes clear why they are important in motivating engagement with a work as well as in describing and sharing texts.

*Promotional.* Promotional elements interface between the work and its potential audience with the goal of making the work appealing to intended readers. Examples of promotional elements include dust jackets, author biographies, endorsements, and award medallions. Promotional elements present another opportunity for readers to decide whether to engage with a work. Peritextual analysis of these elements considers the number and type of promotional elements included in a work and how they influence the potential or actual use of a work.

*Navigational.* Navigational elements assist the reader in understanding the organization of the work and how to search the content. Some examples are the table of contents, index, hyperlinks, and page numbers. Peritextual analysis of these elements can reveal the scope of the work, how topics are arranged, and the author's emphasis or approach to the topic. Navigational elements also reveal how information within the work can be accessed. This guidance is especially important for works that do not have to be experienced linearly, such as reference works or databases. Peritextual analysis can assess how well information is organized and the usability of the work in terms of easy retrieval of information.

*Intratextual.* Intratextual elements interface between the work and the reader by providing insight into what the author was trying to achieve as well as the author's relationship to the work and purpose in creating the work. Some examples of intratextual elements are the foreword, afterword, dedication, and acknowledgments. Peritextual analysis of these elements looks at how they work to increase understanding of the work, to inform ways of approaching the work, and to help the reader understand the purposes for which the work was created.

*Supplemental.* The job of supplemental elements is to provide information outside the main contents of the work to enhance the reader's experience of the text. Some examples of supplemental elements are time lines, maps, photographs, and glossaries. Analysis of these elements can show how they build contextual, historical, linguistic, or other kinds of knowledge as well as how they help the author achieve her goals. Readers can also consider whether there are supplemental materials not contained in the work that would have enhanced the reading experience.

*Documentary.* Documentary elements connect the reader to external materials used in the production of the work as well as to additional materials that support or extend the content of the work. Some examples of documentary elements are source notes, suggested reading, webographies, and reference lists. Readers can use documentary evidence to understand the credibility of a work as well as the sources of the author's knowledge. The presence or absence of documentary elements can affect how the reader engages with a work.

## Significance of Peritext for Teaching and Research

Understanding the functions of peritext and the PLF can offer many benefits to research and teaching. For example, an analysis of peritext can reveal the character and quality of a work and help readers and users decide whether to examine it further. If an individual decides to engage with a work, analyzing peritext can help him understand and appreciate what the work offers.

Peritextual analysis can inform a reader about how a work can be navigated and can reveal the quality of the information in a work before an in-depth reading. It assists the reader in understanding the basis of the author's knowledge as well as what the author is trying to say. Peritext can also be used to clarify discipline-specific use of sources, revealing how knowledge is created within specific learning communities.

Using the PLF as a teaching aid provides librarians and teachers with a structure for teaching critical thinking and increasing reading comprehension. For teachers, the PLF provides a specific approach for teaching critical thinking about a variety of media that can affect the development of skills and dispositions that support critical thinking and information literacy.

Critical thinking is a goal that library and information science and education share in terms of desired outcomes for readers. This goal is embedded in the *Framework for Information Literacy for Higher Education;* the AASL's *National School Library Standards for Learners, School Librarians, and School Libraries;* the *National Assessment of Educational Progress (NAEP)* framework; the *Next Generation Science Standards;* and the *Common Core State Standards.*[10]

As Gross and Latham have noted, the PLF can help students

- Understand how the author has formed an opinion or point of view
- Assess the credibility of information
- Assess the usability of the text
- Assess the ethical dimensions of information used and presented
- Consider how supplemental elements augment presentation of the text
- Develop confidence in interpreting texts
- Consider incorporating peritextual elements into their own writing and design[11]

Students who are able to use the functions of peritext will be able to make better selections of works to engage with, will have a better understanding of a variety of media, and will increase their ability to evaluate the credibility of works. Further, understanding the functions of peritext can support the creation and production of new works across a variety of media.

In addition to using the PLF as a scaffold for critical thinking, teachers can use the framework as a tool for assessing how students are interacting with a work, including their ability to interpret and understand a work, to locate and recall information within a work, and to use peritextual elements to analyze and critique both the credibility and the aesthetic value of a work.

## Sample Applications of the Idea

Although all works incorporate peritext into their production, nonfiction is often a robust source for those interested in mining for peritext. In addition, nonfiction is increasingly being used in classrooms as a way to help students develop the background knowledge needed to support achievement.[12] Thus, initial work on the PLF has utilized nonfiction to test its application to teaching and research. Four applications of the PLF are described next.

*Peritext Book Club: Reading to Foster Critical Thinking about STEAM Texts.*[13] The peritext book club was an after-school activity for sixth- through eighth-graders that was led by the school librarian. The book club's focus was on thinking critically about science, technology, engineering, art, and mathematics (STEAM) texts using the PLF as a framework. The STEAM focus reflects the current emphasis on these topics in schools. Twelve middle school students met once a month for five months to learn about and apply the PLF to various books, one on each of the STEAM topics. Along the way, the students participated in a variety of games developed to teach the functions of peritext and took monthly pre- and post-intervention surveys to track their engagement with the book club and their growing knowledge of peritext. The games were developed by the school librarian using Kahoot! (a free, game-based learning platform) and an interactive whiteboard. The books were all young adult trade books (not textbooks). Over the course of the semester, the students reported enjoying the book club and were able to demonstrate their command of the functions of peritext as well as their understanding of what peritextual elements support these functions. They were also able to demonstrate critical thinking about the books they encountered using the PLF as an evaluation tool.

*Using the Peritextual Literacy Framework with Young Adult Biographies.*[14] This project demonstrated the use of the PLF in the context of a middle school social studies class using the biography *Claudette Colvin: Twice Toward Justice* by Phillip Hoose. The goal of this demonstration was to show content area teachers how the PLF can augment the study of biography in promoting the acquisition of background knowledge and assisting students in navigating the complexity of nonfiction content. The project used a three-pronged approach, using the PLF first as a pre-reading strategy, then during reading, and finally after reading the book. For each phase of reading, the pertinent peritextual functions and elements were discussed and activities suggested for use in the classroom for analyzing the bibliography and extending the work through the creation of extension texts. The researchers also suggested ways in which social studies teachers can work collaboratively with their school librarian to develop lesson plans and assignments, supply resources, assist students in searching for evidence and other resources, help with the integration of technology into lesson plans, and assist with student evaluation.

*Supporting Critical Thinking through Young Adult Nonfiction.*[15] This project focused on the analysis of peritextual elements that help a reader evaluate the credibility of a work: the author biography, author notes, source notes, references, bibliography/webography/discography, suggested reading, and image credits. The researchers used Steve Sheinkin's *Bomb: The Race to Build—and Steal—the World's Most Dangerous Weapon* and Neal Bascomb's *The Nazi Hunt-*

*ers: How a Team of Spies and Survivors Captured the World's Most Notorious Nazi* as case studies. A framework of the following questions taken from Wilson guided the analysis:[16]

- What did the author learn in writing the book?
- How does the author know?
- What sources are used?
- What does the author say about the sources?
- What does the author want us to know about the topic?
- Does the author adhere to documentation standards?

The analysis demonstrated that the authority of these authors relies on providing lists of their previous works rather than indications of their education or special training. The peritextual elements in both books provided information about the process of research and writing and the authors' excitement in working on their projects. Bascomb talked about the quality of his sources and the problem of contradictory accounts. Sheinkin focused on identifying sources he preferred, but not why. Neither work provides the level of source identification that is expected of young adults in school, and image credits in these works were often cited only at the level of the museum, library, or archive where the images reside. These findings provide a basis for an in-depth discussion of how to understand how authors know what they know and how to judge the credibility of works.

*"The President Has Been Shot!"* This case study by Latham, which follows this chapter, identifies and discusses the various types of peritext found in *"The President Has Been Shot!" The Assassination of John F. Kennedy* by James L. Swanson. Further, the chapter provides prompts that can be used in the classroom to assist thinking about how the analysis of peritext aids the reader in approaching, understanding, and evaluating this specific work. This step-by-step guide to a peritextual analysis demonstrates the use of the PLF and provides an example of peritextual analysis that can be followed using other books and media.

## Further Applications and Questions to Consider

Because little has been written about using peritextual analysis to develop critical thinking and information literacy, the topic is rich with opportunities for both research and the development of lesson plans and assessments for use of the PLF in the classroom. The proliferation of media also provides opportunities to further test the PLF and to extend understanding of the presence and absence of peritextual elements in various media types as well as the inclusion of peritext in the production of new works. The question of how peritext can facilitate user experience with media (media literacy) and across media (transliteracy) is far from answered, and the resulting question of how peritext helps users understand, access, navigate, and assess a variety of media should be addressed in research and in work with users across the age spectrum.

Other areas for investigation include research on the usefulness of the PLF for advancing emergent literacy, reading comprehension, reading motivation, and information literacy in formal and informal learning environments. It will also be interesting to learn the extent to which readers who are introduced to the functions of peritext incorporate peritextual analysis into their reading habits and include peritextual elements in the works they produce. This relates also to the need to understand the impact of the functions of peritext on interface design and usability.

As noted throughout this chapter, the PLF is focused solely on the functions of peritext. As a next step in theory development, it will be interesting to explore the functions of epitext and how it influences motivation to read, critical thinking about works, and the interpretation and evaluation of works as well as their reception in the broader culture.

## Conclusion

*Can I do the book club next year again? You'd better do this again next year!*
—Seventh-grade girl

Genette himself notes that the use of paratext (remember, paratext = peritext + epitext) in works is not mandatory and that readers are free to ignore paratext if they wish.[17] However, the importance of paratext has become evident as the number and types of media expand.[18] Peritext is informing research across a wide variety of fields, and it behooves librarians and teachers to explore how students and users can benefit from exposure to the functions of peritext. The PLF fills a gap in paratext theory and provides a scaffold that educators of all kinds can use to promote critical thinking in the use, analysis, and production of works. There is still much to know about how peritext can be harnessed to improve reading comprehension and the development of habits and dispositions that can serve full participation in an increasingly complex world of information. Librarians and teachers have an important role to play in exploring the benefits of peritext in working with students and users of all ages.

## NOTES

1. Melissa Gross, Don Latham, Jennifer Underhill, and Hyerin Bak, "The Peritext Book Club: Reading to Foster Critical Thinking about STEAM Texts," *School Library Research* 19 (October 28, 2016), www.ala.org/aasl/slr.

2. Gérard Genette, *Paratexts: Thresholds of Interpretation* (New York: Cambridge University Press, 1997).

3. Genette, *Paratexts*, 4.

4. Dorothee Birke and Birte Christ, "Paratext and Digitized Narrative: Mapping the Field," *Narrative* 21, no. 1 (2013): 65–87.

5. Paul Benzon, "Bootleg Paratextuality and Digital Temporality: Towards an Alternate Present of the DVD," *Narrative* 21, no. 1 (2013): 88–104; Nadine Desrochers and Daniel Apollon, eds., *Examining Paratextual Theory and Its Applications in Digital Culture* (United States: IGI Global, 2014); Bettina Kummerling-Meibauer, "Paratexts in Children's Films and the Concept of Meta-Filmic Awareness," *Journal of Educational Media, Memory, and Society* 5, no. 2 (2013): 108–23; Ellen McCracken, "Expanding Genette's Epitext/Peritext Model for Transitional Electronic Literature: Centrifugal and Centripetal Vectors on Kindles and iPads," *Narrative* 21, no. 1 (2013): 105–24.

6. Raquel C. Coifman, "Giving Texts Meaning through Paratexts: Reading and Interpreting Endpapers," *School Library Monthly* 30, no. 3 (2013): 21–23; Margaret R. Higonnet, "The Playground of the Peritext," *Children's Literature Association Quarterly* 15, no. 2 (1990): 47–49; Kummerling-Meibauer, "Paratexts in Children's Films," 108–23; Megan D. Lambert, "Gutter Talk and More: Picturebook Paratexts, Illustration, and Design at Storytime," *Children and Libraries* (Winter 2010): 36–42, 46; Miriam Martinez, Catherine Stier, and Lori Falcon, "Judging a Book by Its Cover: An Investigation of Peritextual Features in Caldecott Award Books," *Children's Literature in Education* 47, no. 3 (2016): 225–41; Lawrence R. Sipe, *Storytime: Young Children's Literary Understanding in the Classroom* (New York: Teachers College Press, 2008).

7. Kummerling-Meibauer, "Paratexts in Children's Films," 108–23; Martinez, Stier, and Falcon, "Judging a Book by Its Cover," 225–41.

8. Melissa Gross and Don Latham, "The Peritextual Literacy Framework: Using the Functions of Peritext to Support Critical Thinking," *Library and Information Science Research* 39, no. 2 (2017): 116–23.

9. Sue Thomas, Chris Joseph, Jess Laccetti, Bruce Mason, Simon Mills, Simon Perril, and Kate Pullinger, "Transliteracy: Crossing Divides," *First Monday* 12, no. 12 (2007): 1–2, http://firstmonday.org/ojs/index.php/fm/index.

10. Association of College and Research Libraries, *Framework for Information Literacy for Higher Education* (2016), www.ala.org/acrl/standards/ilframework; American Association of School Librarians, *National School Library Standards for Learners, School Librarians, and School Libraries* (Chicago, IL: ALA Editions, 2017); Institute of Education Sciences, *National Assessment of Educational Progress* (2015), https://nces.ed.gov/nationsreportcard/frameworks.aspx; NGSS Lead States, *Next Generation Science Standards: For States, by States* (2016), www.nextgenscience.org/get-to-know; Common Core State Standards Initiative, *Common Core State Standards for English Language Arts and Literacy in History/Social Studies, Science, and Technical Subjects* (2016), www.corestandards.org/ELA-Literacy/.

11. Gross and Latham, "The Peritextual Literacy Framework," 121.

12. Robert J. Marzano, *A New Era of School Reform: Going Where the Research Takes Us* (Aurora, CO: McREL, 2000).

13. Gross et al., "The Peritext Book Club."

14. Shelbie Witte, Melissa Gross, and Don Latham, "Peritextual Literacy Framework with Young Adult Nonfiction: Navigating Biographies with Adolescents in Social Studies," in *Adolescent Literature as a Complement to the Content Areas: Social Science and Humanities*, ed. Paula Greathouse, Brooke Eisenbach, and Joan F. Kaywell (Lanham, MD: Rowman and Littlefield, 2017), 69–82.

15. Don Latham and Melissa Gross, "Peritext and Pedagogy: Supporting Critical Thinking through Young Adult Nonfiction," in *Options for Teaching YA Literature*, ed. Karen Coats, Roberta Trites, and Michael Cadden (New York: Modern Language Association, forthcoming).

16. Sandip Wilson, "Getting Down to Facts in Children's Nonfiction Literature," *Journal of Children's Literature* 32, no. 1 (2006): 56–63.

17. Genette, *Paratexts*, 4.

18. Thomas Doherty, "The Paratext's the Thing," *Chronicle of Higher Education* 60, no. 17 (2014): B13–B15.

# Peritextual Literacy Framework

| Peritext type | Examples of peritext elements | Consider |
|---|---|---|
| **Production** (Elements that uniquely identify a work) | Author<br>Book designer<br>Copyright<br>ISBN<br>Illustrator<br>Publisher<br>Series title<br>Title (and subtitle)<br>Translator | What do they tell you about the work you have in hand?<br>Where do we find these elements?<br>What uses are there for these elements? |
| **Promotional** (Elements that interface between the work and its potential audience) | Advertisements<br>Author biography<br>Author website URL<br>Award medallions<br>Blurb/bla-bla<br>Dust jacket<br>Endorsements<br>List of other works by author<br>List of other works by publisher<br>List of other works in series | Are they present?<br>How do these elements affect your view of the work?<br>Are they:<br>• Interesting?<br>• Convincing?<br>• Effective? |
| **Navigational** (Elements that assist the reader in understanding the organization of the work and how to search the content) | Chapter divisions<br>Index<br>Intertitles<br>Page numbers<br>Table of contents | How is the information organized?<br>How easy are these elements to use? |

| | | |
|---|---|---|
| **Intratextual**<br><br>(Elements within the work that interface between the work and the reader) | Acknowledgments<br>Afterword<br>Dedication<br>Foreword<br>Preface | Do these increase your understanding of the work?<br><br>Or, make clear the origins or purpose of the work? |
| **Supplemental**<br><br>(Elements outside the text proper that augment understanding of the content) | Pictures<br>Captions<br>Endpapers<br>Glossary<br>Maps<br>Photographs<br>Tables<br>Time line | How do these help you understand the work better?<br><br>Are there elements missing that you wish were there?<br><br>How do these elements help the author make his or her points? |
| **Documentary**<br><br>(Elements that connect the audience to external works used in the production of the work or that reify or extend the content of the work) | Bibliography<br>Discography<br>Image credits<br>References<br>Source notes<br>Suggested reading<br>Webography | Is it clear where the information came from?<br><br>Do they help you understand the author's point of view?<br><br>Do these elements color your impression of the text? |

Source: Melissa Gross and Don Latham, "The Peritextual Literacy Framework: Using the Functions of Peritext to Support Critical Thinking," *Library and Information Science Research* 39, no. 2 (2017): 122.

$$2$$

# Peritext and Young Adult Nonfiction

*A Case Study of "The President Has Been Shot!"*

DON LATHAM

FAR MORE THAN FICTION, NONFICTION BOOKS EMPLOY A RANGE OF PERI-textual elements. Although almost all books, fiction and nonfiction, contain promotional and production peritext, fiction may or may not include navigational and intratextual peritext and rarely includes supplemental and documentary elements. Not only does nonfiction provide a wealth of peritextual elements, but it also encourages a close analysis of those elements in order to evaluate the credentials of the author, the veracity of the sources, and contextual information related to the subject matter. More and more emphasis is being placed on middle school and high school students' ability to read, analyze, and evaluate nonfiction, and mastering those skills begins with developing the ability to successfully recognize and analyze the peritextual elements in nonfiction texts.

## The Text

This chapter presents a case study of one such nonfiction text, James L. Swanson's *"The President Has Been Shot!" The Assassination of John F. Kennedy* (New York: Scholastic Press, 2013). I will briefly summarize the contents of the book, describe the various peritextual elements surrounding the text proper, and discuss how the Peritextual Literacy Framework (PLF) can be used in analyzing this book in a secondary classroom. Swanson's book, which deals with a perennially provocative topic, was published in 2013 on the fiftieth anniversary of Kennedy's murder and was named a Young Adult Library Services Association (YALSA) Excellence in Nonfiction Award finalist. The text proper contains four main sections. A very short Beginnings section sets the stage on a cold, snowy night in January 1961 just before the president-elect's inauguration. Part One: Introduction to John F. Kennedy examines the early years of

Kennedy's political career as well as the major issues of his presidency, including the failed Bay of Pigs invasion, the successful resolution to the Cuban Missile Crisis, the initiation of the Space Race, and the inspirational speech at the Berlin Wall. Part Two: The Assassination constitutes the bulk of the book and provides a day-by-day account beginning with Thursday, November 21, 1963, when the Kennedys left for Texas, and concluding with Monday, November 25, 1963, the day of the funeral. A final Epilogue discusses what happened in the days and months following the assassination, addresses—and dismisses—the various conspiracy theories that have been put forward, and concludes that we may never know why Lee Harvey Oswald assassinated JFK. The book is filled with photographs, all in black and white, along with quotations and eyewitness accounts from the time. It provides almost as much information on Oswald as on Kennedy, and the focus often shifts back and forth between the two. The action-packed narrative reads like a ticking time bomb and is certain to appeal to a wide range of young adult readers.

## The Peritext

Swanson's book provides a wealth of examples of all six peritextual functions designed to encourage reading and enhance the reading experience. Through guided activities, teachers and librarians can help students understand how these peritextual elements work during the pre-reading, reading, and post-reading stages. What follows is an examination of these elements according to function along with some suggested strategies for helping students engage with the various peritextual elements.

*Production.* Production elements include the title, subtitle, author's name, and publication information. The title, subtitle, and author's name appear prominently in three places: the front of the dust jacket, the spine of the dust jacket, and the two-page title page. Publication information is listed on the back (verso) of the right-hand (recto) page of the title page. The publisher's name (Scholastic Press) is listed on the spine of the dust jacket, the left page of the title page, and on the publication page. Other information on the publication page includes contact information for the publisher, the copyright year and provisions, cataloging-in-publication (CIP) data, and book design information (for example, the type fonts and the book designer's name). The ISBN number along with two bar codes appear on the back of the dust jacket. Taken together, this production information uniquely identifies the work, shows how it should be represented in a library catalog, and indicates where it should be shelved in libraries, using either the Dewey Decimal Classification or the Library of Congress Classification system. Anyone wanting to cite this work (for a research paper, for example) would need to know how and where to find this crucial information.

*Production elements in action.* Have students look at the title page and the back of the title page and then answer these questions:

- Who is the publisher of this book? Does the publisher's name mean anything to you?
- When was this book published—what year? Is there any significance to that year in relation to the topic of the book? Explain.

*Promotional.* The promotional elements appear mainly on the dust jacket and consist of two main types: provocative text and images, and author credentials. On the front of the dust jacket, readers are presented with the sensational quotation that also serves as the title, *"The President Has Been Shot!,"* and two iconic photographs. The top photograph, in black and white, shows Oswald in handcuffs with his right hand raised in a clinched fist. (On page 70 of the book, readers learn that this gesture is the Communist salute.) The bottom photograph, in color, shows President and Mrs. Kennedy; he is wearing a suit, and she is dressed in the now famous pink wool suit and pillbox hat. Just peeking up from the lower edge of the photograph are three red roses. (On pages 86–88, readers learn that this photograph was taken at Love Field just before the Kennedys began the motorcade that would take them into downtown Dallas.) The title and subtitle cut across the center of the front cover at a slight angle from upper left to lower right. At the far right of the title is a "spider web" with a hole in the center, as if a bullet has been fired through a glass. (On page 56, readers learn that, although no glass was shattered during the JFK assassination, glass was shattered when Oswald attempted to assassinate former U.S. Army General Edwin Walker.)

Promotional elements continue on the inside front flap of the dust jacket. At the top is another color photograph of the Kennedys, this one of them in the backseat of the presidential open-top limousine that carried them through the streets of Dallas. Kennedy is looking to his right and smiling; Mrs. Kennedy is looking to her left and appears to be smiling as well. Under the photograph, in large, white letters against a dark-red background, are the words, "This is the story of the murder of President John F. Kennedy." Below that is a blurb describing the contents of the book and promising "an action-packed, minute-by-minute, ticking-clock narrative."

The back of the dust jacket features a color image of Oswald, apparently his mug shot, that runs down the entire right side of the back cover. Injuries are evident on his face, and a sign with the prisoner number is partly visible on the left side of the photograph. A blurb summarizing the book's contents appears to the left in white font against a dark-red background. The border around the back cover is black. Interestingly, the blurb on the front flap focuses on the Kennedys and the assassination's profound effect on the nation. In contrast, the blurb on the back cover focuses on Oswald and describes him as neither a fan of JFK's nor a political opponent but, rather, as someone who "wanted to kill the president." The overall intent of the text and images on the front and back covers as well as the front flap is to arouse curiosity by promising a dramatic narrative and ultimately to entice potential readers to purchase or (at least) check out the book.

Other promotional elements emphasize the author's credentials and can be found in various places on the dust jacket as well. On the cover, just below the author's name (which appears under the photograph of Oswald), are the words "Bestselling Author of *Chasing Lincoln's Killer*," connecting the author with another popular young adult nonfiction title. The blurb on the inside front flap emphasizes the point, noting that Swanson is the "award-winning, *New York Times* bestselling author of *Manhunt* and *Chasing Lincoln's Killer*." The back cover of the dust jacket provides excerpts from enthusiastic reviews of *Chasing Lincoln's Killer*, including starred reviews from *Publisher's Weekly* and *School Library Journal*. The fullest accounts of the author's previous works, accolades, educational background, and government positions appear in the author biography on the back flap and in About the Author, which constitutes the last page of the book. Both include the same photograph of Swanson, but the one on the back flap is in color while the one in About the Author is in black and white. In addition, the back flap includes a color thumbnail of the cover of *Chasing Lincoln's Killer*.

The multiple peritextual references to *Chasing Lincoln's Killer* may have a twofold effect. On the one hand, they imply that if Swanson has written one successful book, then he knows how to write an engaging nonfiction narrative. On the other, they suggest that if *"The President Has Been Shot!"* appeals to you, you may find *Chasing Lincoln's Killer* equally appealing. The result, it is hoped, will be that the potential reader will acquire this book and perhaps the other as well. References to Swanson's educational background and government positions are intended to demonstrate that he has both the training and the experience to research and write about an important historical event.

*Promotional elements in action.* Before reading the book, students should be asked to examine the dust jacket, focusing first on the front and back covers. Invite them to look at the front cover and consider these questions:

- Why is the photograph of Oswald at the top of the front cover while the photograph of the Kennedys is at the bottom? What effect does that have on readers?
- Why is Oswald's photograph in black and white and the Kennedys' photograph in color? What effect does that have on readers?
- What do you think of the cover? Does it make you want to read the book? Why or why not?
- Why is the title in quotation marks? (Invite students to compare this title to the titles of other nonfiction books, pointing out that most do not include quotation marks.)

Now ask students to examine the back cover and consider these questions:

- How does the photograph of Oswald on the far right of the back cover compare to the photograph of him on the front cover? Where does the photograph on the back cover seem to have been taken? How can you tell?
- Does reading the blurb about the book make you want to read the book? Why or why not?
- Why do you think the publisher included excerpts from reviews of a different book Swanson wrote (*Chasing Lincoln's Killer*)? Do these excerpts make you want to read *"The President Has Been Shot!"*? Why or why not?

Next, ask students to examine the front flap and back flap of the dust jacket and consider these questions:

- Compare the photograph of the Kennedys at the top of the front flap with the photograph of the Kennedys on the front cover.
- Does the description of the book on the front flap make you want to read the book? Why or why not?
- Why does the publisher want you to know about the author? Does knowing this information affect your desire to read the book? Explain.

*Navigational.* Two sections make up the navigational peritext: the Table of Contents and the Index. The Table of Contents is presented over a two-page spread. A black-and-white photograph of Oswald's view of Elm Street from the sixth-floor window of the Texas Schoolbook Depository is on the left-hand page and continues onto the right. Down the middle of the right-hand page is a column listing the contents of the book, black type against a white background. The Beginnings section is listed along with Part One and Part Two and the Epilogue. Under Part One and Part Two, individual chapter titles are provided. Part One is organized by key events and issues, while Part Two, covering the assassination, is organized chronologically. After the Epilogue is a list of ample peritextual elements in the back matter: Diagrams, Photos, and Illustrations; Places to Visit; Source Notes; For Further Reading; Bibliography; Photo Credits; Index; and Acknowledgments. For whatever reason, the About the Author section, which concludes the book, is not listed. Otherwise the Table of Contents is remarkably complete and provides a clear sense of how the book is organized.

The Index also provides easy access to various topics covered in the book, and on pages where illustrations appear, the page numbers are conveniently printed in boldface. Still, extensive as it is, the Index is not perfect. Those wishing to find references to the home movie of the assassination, for example, might have a bit of trouble, depending on how much prior knowledge they have. Relevant page numbers can be found under "Zapruder, Abraham," of course, but one would need to know the name of the amateur photographer in order to find them. References can be found under other entries as well, such as "Assassination of JFK" and "Media," but still one needs to know Zapruder's last name in order to find the references easily. The brand of camera Zapruder used (a Bell and Howell) is found only under his entry. But no index is perfect, and in all fairness this one appears to be more extensive than most. As is often the case with indexes, this one is most useful to someone who is already familiar with the subject or has already read the book (or both).

*Navigational elements in action.* Ask students to look at the Table of Contents and answer these questions:

- How is the book organized? What are the main parts?
- Which part(s) are you most interested in reading? Why?

Then have students examine the Index and respond to the following:

- Think of a person, event, or thing related to JFK or the assassination or both. See if you can find it in the index.
- Why are some of the page numbers in the index in boldface?

*Intratextual.* Intratextual elements serve as an interface between the work and the reader and may provide information about the origins or purpose of the work. *"The President Has Been Shot!"* contains two such elements—a dedication and an acknowledgments section. The dedication (on page v) reads, "For Andrea and my father, Lennart." It is in white type superimposed over a black-and-white photograph of the interior of (presumably) the sixth floor of the Texas Schoolbook Depository. Presented in white type against a black background, the Acknowledgments section comes just after the Index and just before About the Author. Here Swanson thanks various people who helped as he was writing the book—his family, his agent, the production team at Scholastic, and the like. Of special note are three individuals whom Swanson singles out: Vincent Bugliosi, who wrote "an outspoken and persuasive refutation of the various conspiracy theories that have clouded the history of [the assassination]"; Swanson's mother, who had a closet full of "vintage magazines, illustrated books, newspaper clippings, and photographs" related to the assassination; and his father, who shared his memories from the day Kennedy was shot (pages 272–73). These three individuals, according to Swanson, provided the inspiration for his book. Through the Acknowledgments, readers learn much about the origins of the book as well as Swanson's strong conviction that Oswald acted alone.

*Intratextual elements in action.* At any point in the reading process, ask students to read the Acknowledgments section and then answer the following questions:

- What role did Swanson's mother play in his wanting to write this book?
- What role did Swanson's father play in his wanting to write this book?
- What does Swanson say about conspiracy theories related to the JFK assassination?

Then ask students to flip back to the front of the book and look at the dedication (on page v) and answer this question:

- Given what Swanson says in the Acknowledgments section about his mother's and father's influence on his desire to write this book, why do you think he includes only his father in the dedication?

*Supplemental.* One of the more extensive examples of peritext found in Swanson's book is supplemental, which provides additional information to augment understanding of the topic. There are two sections of supplemental elements in the back matter of the book: Diagrams, Photos, and Illustrations; and Places to Visit. The former contains a number of images and is preceded by an introduction that describes the graphic materials that follow. The illustrations, in the order in which they appear, are (1) a diagram of Oswald's escape route from the Book Depository; (2) diagrams of the rifle, the sight, the clip, and Oswald's position at the sixth-floor window; (3) a diagram of the trajectory of the single bullet that wounded both JFK and Governor John Connally; (4) a diagram depicting Oswald's three shots at JFK; (5) a photograph of the so-called magic bullet that wounded both JFK and Connally; and (6) drawings of JFK's wounds. Although these elements are discussed in the text proper, the supplemental images provide detailed visual information about how the assassination was carried out.

The other section of supplemental information, Places To Visit, is written in prose form with no images and describes places of interest related to Kennedy's life and death. In Dallas, one can visit the Sixth Floor Museum at the old Book Depository building, as well as places where Oswald stayed before or fled to after the assassination. In Washington, D.C., one can see Kennedy's grave at Arlington National Cemetery, the East Room of the White House and the Capitol Rotunda where Kennedy's body lay in state, and the townhouse in Georgetown where the president-elect and his wife lived for a time. In Boston, one can tour the JFK Presidential Library and in nearby Brookline see the home where Kennedy grew up. Though no photographs are included, this section brings the history recounted in the book into the present through vivid descriptions of historical places to see. Strangely, the fact that many of these places have their own websites is not mentioned.

*Supplemental elements in action.* As students are reading the book, especially Part Two on the assassination, ask them to consult the section Diagrams, Photos, and Illustrations and then consider the following questions:

- Which images do you find most useful or interesting or both? Why?
- Do you find any of these images disturbing? Explain.
- Why do you think Swanson and the publisher decided to include these images at the end of the book rather than within the text itself?

Next, have students read the Places to Visit section. They can do this during or after reading the book. Then have them respond to the following:

- Have you visited any of these places? If so, what was it like?
- Which of these places would you like to visit?
- How could you get more information about these places before visiting?

*Documentary.* Documentary elements connect the audience to external works used in the production of the work at hand. Swanson's book contains Source Notes, suggestions For Further Reading, a Bibliography, and Photo Credits, all in the back matter of the book. The source notes are listed in chronological order but are not keyed to specific pages in the text, or even to specific chapters. Instead, key phrases are provided (in boldface), such as "JFK's father" (page 228), "Oswald's rifle" (page 232), and "Filming of the assassination" (page 234). Most of the source notes cite books; for example, in relation to "JFK's father," two biographies of Joseph Kennedy are mentioned, an older one and a more recent one. Full bibliographic citations are provided in what appears to be Modern Language Association (MLA) format. Rarely are specific pages within the books cited, with the exception being references to specific parts of the Warren Report, the official U.S. government report of the investigation into the assassination.

For Further Reading is written in prose (as opposed to being presented as a list) and begins with a meditation on the thousands of published materials on the Kennedy assassination as well as an evocation of the 1960s as a very different time in American society. Swanson recommends consulting original sources from the time, such as newspaper and magazine stories and the U.S. government's official account, the Warren Report. He also recommends several books on the assassination itself, once again discounting the conspiracy books, and he suggests a couple of books on Oswald as well as a couple of books on Kennedy. Though he does not describe his research process, he does offer an evaluation of several of the works he mentions. He writes, for example, "Thomas Mallon's *Mrs. Paine's Garage and the Murder of John F. Kennedy* remains one of my favorite books on the assassination" (page 243). An extensive Bibliography follows, with citations in MLA format and divided into three sections: General References, The Assassination, and Conspiracy Literature. Swanson states here and elsewhere that he does not accept any of the conspiracy theories; nevertheless, he lists twenty-six books one might consult if interested in pursuing this line of inquiry. The Photo Credits, which appear over four pages, are divided into two subsections, Maps and Photos. The items in both subsections are organized chronologically according to the order in which they appear in the book.

The documentary elements in the book serve (at least) three functions. First, they indicate where Swanson obtained his information. If readers wish to do so, they can consult these works themselves to verify the information, although it should be noted that, because Swanson does not provide references to specific page numbers in his sources, tracking down attributions would be tedious and time-consuming. Another function of the documentary elements is to lend authority to Swanson himself. The extensive source notes and bibliography are intended to demonstrate that he has done his homework and that he is a skilled and careful researcher. The third function is to provide direction for additional reading to those wishing to delve further into the various topics covered in the book.

*Documentary elements in action.* After students have finished reading the book, have them closely examine the Source Notes and answer the following:

- Select one source note. Where is the information in Swanson's book that the source note refers to? (Give the page number and paragraph if possible.)
- Considering the same source note, where in the source can the information be found? Can you tell what page the information appears on?
- How do these source notes compare to the way you have cited sources in research papers you have written?

Then ask students to read the For Further Reading section and consider these questions:

- According to Swanson, how were media and communication technologies different in the 1960s compared with today?
- Do you think you would be interested in reading any of the books Swanson mentions? If so, which one(s)?

Have students take a look at the Bibliography and respond to the following:

- How does Swanson organize the Bibliography? What are the subsections?
- Swanson makes it clear that he does not believe the conspiracy theories about the assassination. Why do you think he includes a subsection of books on that topic?

Finally, ask students to examine the Photo Credits section and answer the following questions:

- Why is there a section on photo credits? Isn't it okay to use anything you find online?
- According to the photo credits, what is the source of the photograph of Oswald that appears on the front of the dust jacket?

## Conclusion

There are many options for incorporating the Peritextual Literacy Framework into classroom instruction. This chapter has presented one possible approach, focusing on young adult nonfiction. By encouraging close examination and critical thinking about peritextual elements, teachers and librarians can help students successfully engage with and become more adept readers of nonfiction texts.

# PART II

# STRENGTHENING VISUAL LITERACY THROUGH PERITEXTUAL ANALYSIS

## 3

# Peritextual Bridges

## Predicting Plot and Theme in Boxers & Saints

CRAG HILL

GENE LUEN YANG'S *AMERICAN BORN CHINESE*[1] IS CONSIDERED "A HALLMARK of young adult literature dealing with race and ethnicity"[2] and is thus one of the most commonly taught graphic novels in classrooms from middle school to graduate college. Yang uses the power of image—the mode that can say what words cannot—to illustrate how we can misplace ourselves in our communities. In *American Born Chinese*, the images even more than the text drive the narrative toward insight about how one individual first misplaces then firmly places himself in suburban America, having come to terms with his ethnicity. On the fulcrum of images, *American Born Chinese* leverages issues of identity in contemporary America. A more recent project by Yang, *Boxers & Saints*,[3] uses that same fulcrum to explore identity in a historical setting, far from the United States, with a complex layering of colonialism and its complicated impact—destructive for many but also liberating for some—on the colonized.

This chapter will explore the peritextual elements of Yang's two-volume graphic novel, *Boxers & Saints*, specifically describing a pre-reading lesson using the book covers (together and separate), the book spines (together and separate), and the front and back inside cover flaps to predict the plot of each volume, to examine how the plots of each volume interrelate and contrast with each other, and to help students identify themes within and across the two volumes, as well as providing a view into the two religions depicted in the novels, Christianity and Confucianism (in the form of a Chinese secret society known as the Yihequan, "Righteous and Harmonious Fists"). Along with Lawrence Sipe, who wrote about discussions with children about the peritext of picture books, I believe that "by trusting the book itself to be its own best introduction, then, I mean that thorough discussion of the visual and verbal information on the front and back covers, end pages, title page, and dedication pages is the best preparation for understanding and interpreting the book."[4]

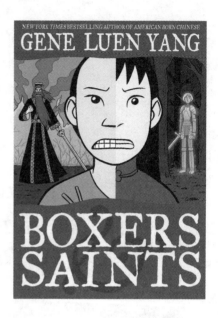

## Crossing Historical and Cultural Gaps

*Boxers & Saints* is a complex text in many ways. Each novel follows a character from before the Boxer Rebellion in China in 1900 to the violent conclusion of the conflict. The first book, *Boxers,* follows the story of Bao, a young boy living in the countryside that has been plagued by bands of foreign missionaries and British soldiers. *Boxers* opens with scenes from Bao's village during a spring fair, including snippets from Bao's favorite pastime, watching Chinese opera. In the scene, he stands as close as he can get to the local earth god, Tu Di Gong, a foot-tall statue, "brought out from his temple and given a seat of honor among the audience."[5] There is much for any reader familiar or unfamiliar with China in the nineteenth century to take in, but in the bombardment of images lies a foreshadowing of the plot. Though the actors who have been representing the Gods of the Opera, including the God of War, depart, the experience has infused Bao with a deep sense of the power of his culture, power that he will tap when his village is threatened by the colonial forces gaining influence in China at the end of the nineteenth century. Bao forms an army of Boxers, peasants trained in kung fu, determined to fight to save China from the foreigners, to protect its millennia-old traditional culture. The first chapter also gives Bao a glimpse of the main character in the second book, Four-Girl, whom he imagines as an elemental power like the Gods of the Opera he has just witnessed.

The second book, *Saints*, covers the adventures and misadventures of Four-Girl, who is spurned by her family, not even given the dignity of a proper name. *Saints*, in its opening pages, has a considerable amount of speech text along with inserts of interior monologue, quotes from the Bible, and symbols of a language Four-Girl cannot understand, presumably English. The opening chapter shows Four-Girl's profound loneliness, her often desperate attempts to have a role in the family. Needing to be a part of something, she becomes captivated by the stories she hears from the local acupuncturist, Dr. Won, who has converted to Christianity, a man who is precariously straddling two cultures. She seeks a place in the world and settles on Christianity, then relatively new to a China that had closed its borders to the West for centuries. When her family discovers she is becoming a disciple of Christianity, she is beaten, and she decides to run away from home.

In both books, it is this complex, changing cultural milieu—the clash of cultures and traditions and its effects on the Chinese people—that students might find is the greatest hurdle to understanding the story. The peritextual elements can provide the bridges for students into these intertwining stories. The images and text on the covers, inside cover flaps, and the book spines give readers clues about the plots and themes of each volume. The covers, flaps, and book spines also point toward the contrasts between the two plots and the thematic connections between the two books. For both books, individually and conjoined, the content of the images invites vigorous speculation about the plots and themes of the novels.

## Theoretical Framework: Visual Literacy

Literacy is more than decoding text or images. "Being literate," Colin Lankshear and Michele Knobel argue, "involves much more than simply knowing how to operate the language systems."[6] Being literate means reading the word (image) and the world,[7] being critically aware of all the sociocultural forces bearing down on the word (image): discourses of gender, class, ethnicity, culture, and social grouping.[8] As the world inexorably shifts from a page-based society to a screen-based society,[9] curriculum is becoming increasingly multimodal. Outside class, students inhabit a multimodal world in which they read, write, make meaning, and communicate with words, images, and sounds in seamless combination.[10]

In the classroom, however, students are primed to glean information about a novel from the kinds of texts that accompany printed books: blurbs on front and back covers and plot-grabbers on the inside cover flaps, front and back, all of which *Boxers & Saints* possesses; students have practiced reading these alphabet-based texts in the classroom since they learned to read. But teachers also need to help students acquire the skills to interpret the images they encounter in their world, in school and out of school. Frank Serafini states this with a sense of urgency: "In order to create an informed and literate citizenry, readers must be able to navigate, interpret, design, and interrogate the written, visual, and design elements of multimodal ensembles."[11] Though our students are immersed in multimodality—as consumers and producers—they aren't always producing and consuming judiciously. A visual literacy curriculum across disciplines could help prepare students to better read their world.

William Kist articulated such a literacy curriculum, one that seamlessly integrates multimodal literacies.[12] He argued that this curriculum will "feature ongoing, continuous usage of multiple forms of representation,"[13] students writing and reading daily in a variety of media. This curriculum will include "explicit discussions of symbol usage currently and throughout history,"[14] explorations of the images students are confronted with in their lives. Because we are all symbol makers and receivers essentially since birth, this curriculum will include instruction on how to critically read and produce symbols, studying symbol use across time and cultures (e.g., the crucifix as it was viewed in the China depicted in *Boxers & Saints*, the symbolism of masks worn in Chinese opera, the mythic stories of warriors in Christianity and China). Throughout this curriculum, students will be expected to think not just in the dominant modes of written and spoken language but also visually, emotionally, and logically. For the lesson introducing the graphic novels to the students, we decided to focus completely on the peritextual elements. We felt the images used on the covers, cover flaps, and spines were particularly evocative of the plots and themes of the at-first two separate and then intertwining stories.

## Teaching Context

*Boxers & Saints* could have a broad readership in social studies and English classes, grades 9–12. The book would better fit in an interdisciplinary class such as world studies, but a teacher of world history could also work with an English teacher to study the novel. The world history class could study the background surrounding the Boxer Rebellion, and the English class could parse the intertwining narratives of Bao and Four-Girl. For this lesson, a university professor worked with a teacher of eleventh- and twelfth-grade English in an alternative high school in a large city on the southern plains.

The classroom was a welcoming space, from the polished wood floors to the shelves packed with individual and class sets of novels, the uncluttered walls, and a large interactive whiteboard in one corner. Students moved to sit in groups at large tables, the teacher greeting them as they entered the room. Ten students were in attendance, six females and four males. One student had a bilingual aide assisting him. All students were prepared to work and maintained attention and kept pace with the lesson to the end of the period. *Boxers & Saints* was the first graphic novel in the class. The class library included many graphic novels, but only one of the students had selected them previously for her independent reading. This would be the first time that students had worked explicitly with the peritextual elements before reading a whole class text.

## Predicting Plot and Identifying Themes

This lesson was a pre-reading exercise that focused on predicting plot and themes based on the images and text on the covers, the cover flaps, and the book spines. Throughout the reading of the novels, readers could return to these images to expand their understanding of plot and theme, thinking closely about how the peritextual images frame the two books and how they contribute to meaning.

*Step 1: The Covers.* The front covers give readers a clue about the plots and themes. On *Boxers*, the right side of Bao's face is in the foreground. He has a fierce expression. Behind him a tall, bearded man, fist clenched, sword at the ready, stands before a wall of flames consuming a forest in the background. This man, we find out later, is depicted as Ch'in Shih-huang, The First Divine Sovereign, who forged China "from the blood and spirits of seven warring kingdoms!"[15] "With my own fist," he tells Bao, "I brought her righteousness and harmony!"[16] On the cover of *Saints*, in a dark wood (perhaps the forest engulfed in flames on the cover of Boxers), a figure stands in full armor, holding a sword. The figure is calm, looking off and up into space. The left side of Four-Girl's face appears in the foreground on the left side of the cover. Four-Girl, who eventually takes the Christian name Vibiana, has a fierce expression that matches Bao's.

We asked students to view the covers individually, first *Boxers*, then *Saints*, and to jot down what they thought the novel would be about, what its themes would be. These are some of the responses students wrote after viewing the cover of *Boxers*: "It looks like there might be evil. They [the right side of Bao's face and Ch'in Shih-huang] want to defeat something or someone." Another student predicted that the book would be about "fighting a master," that the figure in the background "may be of fire," that the two characters on the cover "may dislike one another," and that "there will be sword fighting." One student wrote based on the cover that *Boxers* would be about "a kid who is trained by his master," predicting that Ch'in Shih-huang is Bao's master and will train him for battle. It is, in fact, as we find out in the book, Ch'in Shih-huang's form that Bao takes in battle.

For *Saints*, one student wrote that the character on the cover, whom he misidentified as a male, "will find someone who trains him better." Another wrote that the ghostlike figure in the background is "the ghost of a knight come back for revenge or justice." Another student wrote that the character on the cover (whom she identified as female) "looks scared" but that "there's a guy in the back that looks like he might save something or someone." We find out later that the figure is a vision of Joan of Arc who indeed influences Four-Girl to establish her identity as a faithful Christian. Another student observed that the figure is "the knight to save China."

We then asked students to view the covers together (the faces conjoined) and to jot down what they think the two novels together would be about. One student wrote, "The characters might be going against each other. One wants evil and one wants no evil. It's like bad versus good." Another student concurred that the two stories would be about "the struggle between bad and good." Another wrote, "I think they're going to come together about how something bad happens, then it turns good." These responses demonstrate a growing insight into one of the most important themes of the two books: good versus evil.

After sharing in table groups, the main points we collected on the board were that *Boxers* would be about evil, that it would involve an emperor who is trying to take back what was his from foreigners threatening China, and that there would be lots of arguing and fighting. Collectively, students felt that *Saints* would be a contrast to *Boxers*, a story about peace where good things will happen. One student predicted that the character on the cover of *Saints* would fall in love with "the shining figure." Though it is not a romantic love, it could be argued that Four-Girl, who in *Saints* chooses the name Vibiana, indeed has a platonic love for the figure (a vision of Joan of Arc we eventually find out, recognized as a heroine of the Hundred Years' War, later canonized as a Roman Catholic saint), a love that drives Vibiana's decisions in the plot and thematic climax of *Saints*, her decision not to renounce her Christian faith even when confronted by harm.

From viewing the covers, students formulated strong initial impressions about the two stories and how they related to each other. These predictions were posted and revisited throughout the reading of the novels, with further reading fleshing out what is "good" or "bad" in each of the novels, who is fighting for what, and what are the root causes for each of the characters as they take action for what they feel is right.

*Step 2: Inside Cover Flaps.* The contrast—and connections—between the two plots and themes is also evident in the inside cover flaps. On the front cover flap of *Boxers*, a dozen men—or gods?—fly toward battle, swords and spears drawn. On the back cover flap, two men with traditional cues (long hair bound in a single braid), arms crossed, watch the sun rise—or set—over a small village. On the front flap, the glowing figure in *Saints* is now on a horse leading a group of armed men past a house from which Four-Girl watches. On the back flap, Four-Girl is approaching a church with a man out front sweeping the ground. The text on the flaps provides a few specific details that help readers make sense of the images, including information about what is happening to Bao's village and other villages like his and a brief summary of Four-Girl's home life.

We asked the students to read and view the inside cover flaps individually, first *Boxers*, then *Saints*, and to jot down anything they could add to their predictions of plot and theme. For *Boxers*, students increased their understanding of the conflict between foreign missionaries and soldiers and Bao's motivation for an armed rebellion because many of the men in his region have been killed or tortured by soldiers enforcing their rules and by the Christian missionaries determined to wipe out the spiritual beliefs of the villagers, which they view as superstition. One student wrote that Bao and other men from his region "fight for the glory of China. They [learned] kung fu to beat the devils." Another student noted that "soldiers roamed around bullying," and another wrote that "the book is really about China being bullied and robbed and a war starts to protect China." Another student stated that Bao is "a young man [who] has had enough and puts together an army of 'Boxer' or kung fu fighters." For Saints, one student noted that the novel is about a "girl torn between two worlds, her choices that kept her pure but still fighting for what she believes in." Vibiana, formerly Four-Girl, another student writes, is "a girl [who] wasn't given a proper name and she found one with her Christian friends. They are also fighting for the right to be Christians."

After sharing in table groups, the main point we collected on the board was that the two novels would play out a conflict between worldviews, a conflict that erupts in violence perpetrated by both sides. Students noted that *Boxers* would be about fighting for China against the forces trying to eradicate its traditional culture. *Saints* would be about a girl's quest to be someone, to have value in her life and world, something she was denied in her village because of traditional culture.

From reading and viewing the cover flaps, from writing and talking about their findings, students demonstrated their initial understanding of the conflicts between the Boxers and those from foreign countries working in China, and, more important, this peritextual material began to reveal to these readers what motivates Bao and Vibiana to action in their narratives.

*Step 3: The Spines.* When the spines of both books are joined by the ampersand (*Boxers & Saints*), the two halves of the faces come together as one, suggesting that these two stories have two sides, that there is more than one way to look at a conflict between people and cultures. Because of time constraints, we were not able to complete this step. In implementing this pre-reading lesson in the future, we would start with viewing, writing about, and discussing the two spines together. For one, they show what the characters have in common—an anger about the current state of their worlds—and might also help students identify the genders of the two characters and help students begin to think about the characters' differences.

## Conclusion

We believe that these supplementary peritextual elements were well designed by the publisher to suggest the plot and evoke the themes of the two books. We also believe that the inherent nature of graphic novels—images carrying as much if not more of the meaning than words—enhances the effectiveness of peritextual materials. This pre-reading exercise piqued the curiosity of students for reading *Boxers & Saints* and through image and text helped build the background knowledge that students needed to make thoughtful interpretations of the stories of two compelling characters and their very different worldviews, two young people who cross paths in a turbulent time for each and for the China they have grown up in. This pre-reading exercise guided readers to think not only about historical events but also about the ways that different worldviews contributed to these events. Both narratives are ultimately bound together by the drive we all share to have a purpose in the world, now and in the future, within the boundaries of a nation or the belief in faith without boundaries.

### NOTES

1. Gene Luen Yang and Lark Pien, *American Born Chinese* (New York: First Second, 2006).

2. Mike Cadden, "'But You Are Still a Monkey': American Born Chinese and Racial Self-Acceptance," *The Looking Glass: New Perspectives on Children's Literature* 17, no. 2 (2014), http://bravo.lib.latrobe.edu.au/ojs/index.php/tlg/article/view/477/427.

3. Gene Luen Yang and Lark Pien, *Boxers & Saints* (New York: First Second, 2013).

4. Lawrence Sipe, "Learning from Illustrations in Picturebooks," in *Teaching Visual Literacy: Using Comic Books, Graphic Novels, Anime, Cartoons, and More to Develop Comprehension and Thinking Skills,* ed. Nancy Frey and Doug Fisher (Thousand Oaks, CA: Corwin Press, 2008), 142.

5. Yang and Pien, *Boxers & Saints,* 3.

6. Colin Lankshear and Michele Knobel, *New Literacies: Changing Knowledge and Classroom Learning* (Buckingham [England]: Society for Research into Higher Education/Open University Press, 2003), 12.

7. Paulo Freire and Donald Macedo, *Literacy: Reading the Word and the World* (London: Routledge and Kegan Paul, 1987).

8. Colin Lankshear, with James P. Gee, Michele Knobel, and Chris Searle, *Changing Literacies, Changing Education,* ed. Andy Hargreaves and Ivor Goodson (Buckingham [England]: Open University Press, 2002).

9. Gunther Kress and Theo Van Leeuwen, *Multimodal Discourse: The Modes and Media of Contemporary Communication* (London: Arnold, 2001).

10. Donna Alvermann, "Why Bother Theorizing Adolescents' Online Literacies for Classroom Practice and Research?," *Journal of Adolescent and Adult Literacy* 52, no. 1 (2008), 8–19; Donna Alvermann, ed., *Adolescents' Online Literacies: Connecting Classrooms, Digital Media, and Popular Culture* (New York: Peter Lang, 2010).

11. Frank Serafini, *Reading the Visual: An Introduction to Teaching Multimodal Literacy* (New York: Teachers College Press, 2014), 16.

12. William Kist, "Beginning to Create the New Literacy Classroom: What Does the New Literacy Look Like?," *Journal of Adolescent and Adult Literacy* 43 (2000): 710–18.

13. Kist, "Beginning to Create," 712.

14. Kist, "Beginning to Create," 713.

15. Yang and Pien, *Boxers & Saints*, 157.

16. Yang and Pien, *Boxers & Saints*, 157.

APPENDIX

# Resources

For educators interested in teaching *Boxers & Saints*, the following resources will be of interest.

- For background on Christianity in China at the time of *Boxers & Saints*, visit Frontline's 2008 story, "Jesus in China: Is Christianity Transforming China?" The *Frontline* web page "A Brief History of Christianity in China" (www.pbs.org/frontlineworld/stories/china_705/history/china.html) includes a reference to a Christian convert named Hong Xiuquan, who claimed to be the younger brother of Jesus Christ. Four-Girl's father ran away from home and joined Hong Xiuquan's movement, the Heavenly Kingdom of Transcendent Peace, which included an armed rebellion against Qing Dynasty rulers that lasted fifteen years, resulting in the loss of millions of lives before the Chinese imperial army with the aid of Western military advisors put down the rebellion.
- For exploration before reading the novels—or as enrichment after reading—complete the mask-making shown in the "Lesson on Beijing Opera," produced by the Confucius Institute at the University of Oklahoma (http://ouci.publishpath.com/Default.aspx?shortcut=beijingopera). The lesson includes templates for many different masks.
- For more on Ch'in Shih-huang (Qín Shǐ Huángdì 秦始皇帝), the first emperor of China, read the online *National Geographic* article "Emperor Qin's Tomb" and view the video of the now-famous terracotta warriors discovered in 1974 (https://www.nationalgeographic.com/archaeology-and-history/archaeology/emperor-qin/).
- For other instructional suggestions, visit Meryl Jaffe's "Using Graphic Novels in Education: *Boxers & Saints*" (http://cbldf.org/2013/10/using-graphic-novels-in-education-boxers-saints/). One group of suggestions is titled "The Power of Cultural Heritage, Faith, and Perspective" and includes ideas such as charting "the positive things the Boxers and the Saints did for their respective communities. Then chart the negative things they did to others as they responded to feelings of

humiliation and persecution. Discuss who the 'winners' and 'losers' are—if any exist at all." The page also includes detailed background and plot summaries for both novels.

- Because Joan of Arc is a significant secondary character in *Saints*, it is important that students learn about her life and accomplishments. For a brief overview of Joan of Arc, an article on the website for the History Channel is one place to start (www.history.com/topics/saint -joan-of-arc). The *Encyclopedia Britannica* has a more extensive biography, including images of Joan (the only portrait done of her in her lifetime) and videos, such as "Research into Joan of Arc's Appearance" (https:// www.britannica.com/biography/Saint-Joan-of-Arc).

$$\bigcirc\!\!\!\!4$$

# Book Speed Dating and the
# Art of Making Lasting Connections

JILL SLAY

**AS IS A USUAL OCCURRENCE, A STUDENT ENTERS THE LIBRARY, ACCOMPANIED** by a teacher, an administrator, or a staff member, looking for a book for the first time ever. Nate, a sophomore, was the student on this day.

"I'll be honest, Ms. Slay, I've never been in here before. I just need a book while I sit in the office."

Thus begins a normal day in the life of an inner-city school librarian: matching a kid, who is a self-identified nonreader, not a patron of the library, a kid who is happy to be spending his day in the office rather than taking a practice ACT, with a book that will interest him enough to keep him out of trouble in the office. Three books are pulled for him: *Ready Player One* by Ernest Cline, *When I Was the Greatest* by Jason Reynolds, and *Hoops* by Walter Dean Myers, three books that typically appeal to reluctant, male readers.[1] Nate's eyes light up when he sees the cover for *When I Was the Greatest*. "It has a pistol on it. That must be good, right?" He picks it up, checks it out, reads it for the day, asks the main office secretary if she will hold on to it so he does not lose it, and finishes it the next day. The only thing he knew about it was that it had a pistol on the cover. This scenario illustrates the Peritextual Literacy Framework (PLF) in action, even on a subconscious level. In this instance, the student analyzed the cover to predict interest, to create a connection, and to interact with the text in order to choose what book he thought would hold his attention for the next two days.

Teenagers today are exposed to visual images from the second they are born. On average, students between the ages of 13 and 19 spend approximately nine hours per day using media for enjoyment.[2] This translates to thousands of interactions with visual images every day. Teens routinely connect to their world through social media, which is dominated by visual images. Being able to decipher these images is essential to their understanding of the world in which they operate, and beyond. Their ability to "create, critique, analyze, and evaluate multimedia texts" is vital for them to be successful in understanding 21st century literacies, as they are defined by the National Council of Teachers of English (NCTE).[3] Although taking in visual images is innate to teenagers, being able to process that information intentionally to make informed decisions and to understand texts still has to be explicitly taught. Visual literacy is defined by the International Society for Technology in Education (ISTE) as "the ability to understand, interpret, and evaluate visual messages."[4] As standards evolve in an ongoing effort to better prepare students for the twenty-first century, so must students' understanding of "print and non-print texts in relationship to themselves as readers," especially when it comes to reading for pleasure.[5] Implementing the Peritextual Literacy Framework, in a way that allows students to address and assess the subtleties of book covers, can help young people develop critical thinking and visual literacy skills. Being able to think critically and anticipate a connection to a text can, ultimately, result in fewer reluctant readers and more thoughtful, informed, invested readers.[6]

## Context

I am the sole librarian in an inner-city high school attended by students who are primarily low income and members of minority groups. This school is located in the southern plains of the United States and serves 1,600 students in ninth through twelfth grades. Our students have limited access to resources or support. Many of these students have hopes of attending college and would be the first in their families to do so. Some students work to pursue a vocational career. They want to create a better life for themselves than they currently have. Preparing them for their lives beyond high school is vital for their success, and cultivating an environment that celebrates 21st century literacies and fosters a love of reading is the ultimate goal of the school. However, creating a culture of reading and learning can be an uphill struggle. Many of our students do not have home access to the Internet, books, or public libraries. Their only access is what the school library can offer. They are dependent on the school to meet their academic needs. Teachers and administrators work hard and are constantly looking for tools to develop skills that will translate to success in college and career. The faculty explores strategies and collaborates to embed 21st century literacies in the curriculum. Implementing strategies like the PLF is a way to help students make sense of texts and the world around them.

## Statement of Problem

In 2002, the U.S. Census Bureau, in conjunction with the National Endowment for the Arts (NEA), surveyed 17,000 Americans regarding their participation in the arts, including reading literature. The findings were dire, resulting in a publication entitled *Reading at Risk*.[7] This survey showed that the number of people who participate in leisure reading—reading done outside work or school—has been steadily declining since 1982. The demographic exhibiting the steepest decline is young people ages 18–24. According to the NEA's findings, "The accelerating declines in literary reading among all demographic groups of American adults indicate an imminent cultural crisis."[8] The effects on a society in which people are less literate can include lower wages, lower intellect, and a less vibrant and effective democracy, to name a few. And although a follow-up document, *Reading on the Rise*, in 2008, showed that reading among adults was increasing, the decline in teenage leisure reading is reinforced with the Common Sense Media survey done in 2014.[9] In contrast, a Pew Research Center study conducted in 2012 found that teenagers were the demographic most likely to visit a library, prompted by research or reading assignments.[10] Because high school students are "especially reliant on the library for their reading and research needs," libraries have an opportunity to connect with young people and develop their interests in leisure reading. As a result, teachers and librarians need to tap into this connection and try to "sell" reading for pleasure. How can they do that? By teaching their students how to assess, understand, and connect with literature using the PLF created by Melissa Gross and Don Latham. Teachers and librarians can use visual literacy skills that students develop through participating on social media.[11]

Book covers are, essentially, a book's profile picture. They are the first interaction a student has with a text and can dictate a student's willingness to pick
up the book and explore it. Librarians play an essential role in creating this connection between text and reader, an influence that cannot be understated. The
American Association of School Librarians (AASL) states that one role of the
school librarian is to "practice responsive collection development and support
print-rich environments that reflect the curriculum and the diverse learning
needs of the school community."[12] Therefore, the PLF must be considered when
developing a collection in order to create connections between readers and
texts in an effort to create lifelong readers. In addition to collection development, it is imperative that librarians create lessons and activities that illustrate
how students can connect with literature and make informed decisions.

## Theoretical Framework and Review of Relevant Literature

In this digital age, AASL has created new standards in an effort to ensure that
librarians teach their students how to sharpen their media literacy skills.[13]
Visual literacy is only one aspect of media literacy. Common Sense Media
defines media literacy as "the ability to identify different types of media and
understand the message they are sending."[14] In order for students to be intelligent consumers of information, they need to think critically about the messages they encounter and use that critical thinking to make informed, well-
thought-out decisions. This twenty-first-century skill not only is essential for
college or career but is a necessary life skill as well.

Honing these skills should start as early as possible. In school, one approach
that teachers and librarians have at their disposal is the Peritextual Literacy
Framework. The PLF is an extension of Genette's theory on paratextual analysis and was developed by Melissa Gross and Don Latham.[15] Organizing peritextual features into six categories, the PLF provides educators with multiple
avenues for teaching students to analyze texts and media messages. Teachers
and librarians are beginning to use the PLF as a scaffolding tool to help students become more adept at analyzing visual images and, thus, become more
effective readers and consumers of information.

In 2006, researchers Lawrence Sipe and Caroline McGuire focused on analyzing endpapers in picture books as a way to help elementary students understand the importance of peritextual features.[16] By emphasizing that all peri-

textual features are a design choice, the researchers encouraged children to use those choices to draw inferences, think critically, and develop questions about texts before they read. According to Sipe and McGuire, when teachers "discuss picture books with children, [they] should make them aware that every element in the book is meaningful and worthy of interpretation."[17] Allowing for this kind of interpretation invites deep discussions about texts that can broaden children's critical thinking and inference-making skills.[18]

Leading a research team in 2016, Florida State University professor Melissa Gross introduced a group of students to the PLF.[19] Gross's book club focused on the PLF as it relates to nonfiction and devoted a meeting to each of the six categories: promotional, bibliographic (later changed to production), navigational, intratextual, supplemental, and documentary. The hope was that the PLF would be an effective tool for teaching media literacy skills. Students found the promotional and intratextual materials to be the easiest to identify and analyze. When discussed in conjunction, these two categories markedly increased a student's motivation to engage with a text.[20] In some cases, analyzing only the promotional elements led students to not want to read a book; however, if they delved more into the intratextual elements, they felt more compelled to read the book.

All the articles focusing on the PLF as a conduit for analyzing messages introduced similar findings. The more students understood the peritextual features, the more motivated they were to read the text. By 2014, the number of students who said they "never" or "hardly ever" read had tripled since 1984.[21] In this same study, 45 percent of 17-year-olds said they read for pleasure only once or twice per year. The decline in reading has been a steady march, and the culprits are increased use of technology, longer working hours for parents, and increased homework. This decline in reading has forced libraries to evolve and to appeal to students on a visual level. Therefore, the PLF is an essential tool for librarians to use to appeal to students' visual understanding.

In June 2007, *School Library Journal* published Leigh Ann Jones's article, "The Great Cover Up: Do Kids Judge Books by Their Cover?," which outlined an informal study Jones conducted at her middle school in Texas. She surveyed 608 sixth- through eighth-graders and found that book covers are the "number one factor that impact the selection of fiction books" regardless of gender or age.[22] Publishing houses spend a great deal of effort creating the perfect book cover. Librarians develop parts of their collections based on cover art. Covers are an integral part of the book design process. Providing students with tools to consider, understand, and analyze these covers will provide them with opportunities to think critically, internalize their own preferences, and become more independent and thoughtful consumers of information. Societies with thoughtful, literate consumers create higher functioning democracies, higher wage jobs, and a stronger culture of empathy.

Neil Gaiman gave a speech at the Reading Agency annual meeting in October 2013, emphasizing the importance of having a literate society, a society that is more thoughtful, more empathetic, more exploratory, more creative and inventive. He emphasized the importance of libraries as places to communicate, to grow as learners, and to access, not just books but information. But mostly, he emphasized that in order to raise literate children, one must "teach them to read, show them that reading is a pleasurable activity, and that means, at its simplest, find books that they enjoy, give them access to these books, and let them read them."[23] The first step in this relationship with books usually comes down to the cover.

## Practical Methods and Application of Ideas

In an effort to create lifelong readers and learners, a team including administrators, classroom teachers, students, and myself worked to implement a schoolwide reading initiative. Students have vastly different needs and interests when it comes to reading. Most of the students the library serves are struggling and reluctant readers. Therefore, developing a collection that will appeal to them is a daunting task, but fortunately the faculty is proactive when it comes to creating readers. Two teachers, Mrs. Paul and Mrs. Woosley, were willing to bring their classes to the library and be a part of the speed dating activity in an effort to match students with books that they would enjoy reading. Mrs. Paul teaches sophomore English, and Mrs. Woosley teaches junior English. Both classes are on level, and both teachers allowed me the opportunity to teach their classes the PLF.

Full disclaimer: speed dating is not a new concept in the secondary school library. This activity was adapted by using the bones of speed dating as a way to facilitate instruction in the PLF. This activity focused on the production and promotional aspects of the PLF. Speed dating consists of giving students a short amount of time to interact with books in an effort to make a connection. Mrs. Paul's and Mrs. Woosley's classes participated in speed dating twice:

once preceding PLF instruction and once after implementing the PLF. Stacks of books were placed on tables, and students were allotted three minutes to look at the books and choose one from each table that they would be interested in reading. Initially, students struggled to come up with one from each table. They were not clear on what to look for, how to assess the covers of the books, what connections could be made. A few students checked out books. A smaller number of students got really excited about the books they checked out. For a librarian in an inner-city school, this still feels like a win.

The next time the students came to the library, they participated in a large-group discussion focused on analyzing visual images. Students viewed movie posters and still photos from popular movies and TV shows: *Wonder Woman*, *It*, *Stranger Things*. In groups, they made lists of what they knew about the movies and shows, then they connected details from the images as evidence of what they knew. They included plot details such as setting, characters, even theme. Students discussed how they were given clues to the text from the promotional and production elements of the text. Next, students were shown images of movies and TV shows that they would not be familiar with: the original *Superman*, *Stand By Me*, *The Wonder Years*. The students then predicted what these shows were about and found details in the images that supported their predictions. The discussion then moved on to book covers. For this large-group discussion, *Drama* by Raina Telgemeier and *Victory: Resistance Book 3* by Carla Jablonski and Leland Purvis were used.[24] Students listed details that they noticed and then predicted some of the same plot elements and what they thought the book would be about. They had a stack of books at their tables, and they did the same work in small groups. Then it was time for Speed Dating: Round Two.

This time around, students knew how to look for details and to connect those details to plot elements, making them better equipped to make informed decisions about how they would enjoy the book. The students' comments and handouts painted a clear picture. Using the PLF to analyze the covers of their books, they were able to more accurately gauge their interest in books based on the covers. At the conclusion of round two, only seventeen students out of 270 did not connect with a book. Students were excited about the books they selected. They felt energized by the experience.

> Janiyah (junior): "This was fun. I didn't really know what I was looking at the first time, but I know I made a good choice today. I am excited to read *Dumplin.*"

Charles (sophomore): "Usually I just read the same books over and over because I don't know what else sounds good, but *Ready Player One* looks really good. I love gaming and am into virtual reality."

Student handouts illustrated a more sophisticated understanding of how to look for details to choose a book that is interesting. In round one, there were a lot of "I don't know" and "I don't like books" responses, but in round two, there were a lot more references to specific details and to why those details appealed or did not appeal to the student. This higher level of engagement and understanding in round two is illustrated by the side-by-side comparison of one student's work in figure 4.1.

Students consistently mentioned that it was fun to get to interact with different books that they would not normally pick up. In her round two handout, Caitlyn wrote about not enjoying graphic novels, but the two she chose

**FIGURE 4.1**

**Comparison of speed dating responses**

Speed Dating with Books

Name _Caitlyn_
Round 1

| | Title | Author | Rating | Notes |
|---|---|---|---|---|
| 1 ① | Cy in Chains | Dudley | ♥ ☺ 😐 😟 | I don't know, looks boring |
| 2 | | | ♥ ☺ 😐 😟 | |
| 3 ② | If I Was Your Girl | Russo | ♥ ☺ 😐 😟 | looks okay, a romance w/a transgendered person |
| 4 | | | ♥ ☺ 😐 😟 | |
| 5 ③ | This Is Where it Ends | Nijkamp | ♥ ☺ 😐 😟 | looks too intense |
| 6 | | | ♥ ☺ 😐 😟 | |
| 7 ④ | Playbook | Alexander | ♥ ☺ 😐 😟 | I'm into sports, so ok |
| 8 | | | ♥ ☺ 😐 😟 | |
| 9 ⑤ | Dumplin' | Murphy | ♥ ☺ 😐 😟 | Beauty Queens - Not my thing |
| 10 | | | ♥ ☺ 😐 😟 | |
| 11 ⑥ | Forever Man | Colfer | ♥ ☺ 😐 😟 | Never read the series |
| 12 | | | ♥ ☺ 😐 😟 | |
| 13 ⑦ | Passengers | Bracken | ♥ ☺ 😐 😟 | No thanks |
| 14 | | | ♥ ☺ 😐 😟 | |
| 15 | | | ♥ ☺ 😐 😟 | |
| 16 | | | ♥ ☺ 😐 😟 | |
| 17 | | | ♥ ☺ 😐 😟 | |
| 18 | | | ♥ ☺ 😐 😟 | |
| 19 | | | ♥ ☺ 😐 😟 | |
| 20 | | | ♥ ☺ 😐 😟 | |

intrigued her. She would normally not even look in the graphic novel section, but she checked out *Drama* as her backup. When asked further about her choice, she mentioned that the cover presented a love triangle that takes place in a theater setting. As a student who participates in her school's drama department, she found this aspect appealing.

To reinforce the analysis skills used in this activity, students were asked to create "covers" using only a blurb of the book. Students had to incorporate details from the text into their cover in order to convey some of the book's plot elements. Students found this exercise difficult because they were not given their choice of book. Instead, each student was handed a book at random. As a result, many students had no personal connection to the text they were assigned. Because the goal was to have students focus on the details in the blurb rather than use their background knowledge, this random distribution was an attempt to limit the number of students who had previous experience with the

**FIGURE 4.1 (continued)**
**Comparison of speed dating responses**

Speed Dating with Books — Name: Caitlyn — Round 2

| | Title | Author | Rating | Notes |
|---|---|---|---|---|
| 1 ① | How to Hang a Witch | Mather | | looks ok, not really my |
| 2 | | | | interest |
| 3 * ② | Lab Girl | Hope Jahren | | I love science + Nature |
| 4 | | | | tree + twenyur!!?? |
| 5 ③ | Drama | Telemeier | | I don't usually read |
| 6 | | | | graphic novels, but |
| 7 | | | | I ALWAYS have drama, Lol |
| 8 ④ | A Long Way Down | J. Reynolds | | I see an elevator, but I'm |
| 9 | | | | still not sure what it means. |
| 10 ⑤ | What We Become | Perez-Roerto | | They are dancing. A Romance |
| 11 | | | | maybe?, I'd read this. |
| 12 * ⑥ | Wonder Woman | Leigh Bardugo | | I ♡ Wonder Woman so |
| 13 | Warbringer | | | this is awesome! |
| 14 | | | | |
| 15 ⑦ | March: Book 1 | John Lewis | | Another Graphic Novel, I |
| 16 | | | | have studying Civil Rights |
| 17 | | | | so this might be cool. |
| 18 | | | | |
| 19 | | | | |
| 20 | | | | |

book they were drawing about. Students also found it challenging to not be influenced by the existing cover, and many tried to re-create what they saw. Charles, a sophomore, created his interpretation of *Long Way Down* by Jason Reynolds.[25] Charles focused on the setting of the elevator but wanted to include the detail of the gun to highlight the tone of violence in the blurb (figure 4.2).

**FIGURE 4.2**
**Student version of a book cover**

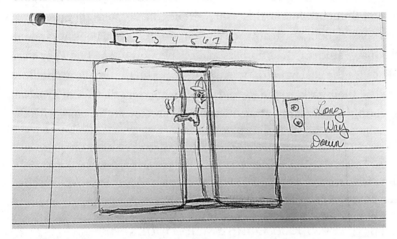

## Further Applications

Using book covers as a conduit to understanding tone is another way that students can be successful, especially in classrooms that focus on analyzing literature. Using book covers to identify tone in the Advanced Placement (AP) classroom taps into students' already-developed visual literacy in an effort to shore up their ability to recognize tone in text. In Mrs. Gateley's AP English Literature class, seniors were introduced to the PLF as an additional tool to identify tone. In an inner-city school, with high populations of underrepresented minorities, it is mandatory to tap into students' background knowledge to teach higher level analysis skills. Thus, because students are more comfortable processing visuals, it makes sense to start there. Students are more adept at recognizing details that contribute to tone in images than in text, so to teach tone, the place to start is visual art. For this activity, students looked at *The Scream* by Edvard Munch, *The Starry Night* by Vincent van Gogh, and *American Gothic* by Grant Wood. Students identified the tone and listed details from the paintings as evidence (figure 4.3). Then they moved on to book covers: *Lord of the Flies* by William Golding, *Frankenstein* by Mary Shelley, and *The Handmaid's Tale* by Margaret Atwood.[26] Students completed the same activity using only the book covers. Using the PLF to identify the overall tone of a text helps students be more mindful and aware of the evidence within the text that reinforces that tone. For example, as shown in figure 4.4, students identified details from the book cover for Golding's *Lord of the Flies* and then went on to brainstorm tone words based on those details. This same process was then applied to passages from the text.

**FIGURE 4.3**

**Details and tone words from *American Gothic***

**FIGURE 4.4**

**Details and tone words from *Lord of the Flies***

## Conclusion

Incorporating the PLF into the library and classroom helps students connect to books, and reading, in a more meaningful way. Because recreational reading is on the decline, teachers and librarians need to be more creative in the ways that they connect readers and texts. Helping students develop the raw skills that they already possess as a way to make informed and knowledgeable decisions about books is becoming more necessary as students are finding more and more reasons to not be readers. Additionally, using book covers to reinforce students' skills in analyzing visual images reinforces visual literacy, which is essential for success in the twenty-first century. Giving students the PLF is a step in the right direction to increase the number of students who read, to incorporate thoughtful and insightful analysis in the texts they read, and to cultivate intelligent and contemplative consumers of information.

### NOTES

1. Ernest Cline, *Ready Player One* (New York: Broadway Books, 2012); Jason Reynolds, *When I Was the Greatest* (New York: Atheneum Books for Young Readers, 2015); Walter Dean Myers, *Hoops* (New York: Ember Reprint, 2012).

2. Kelly Wallace, "Teens Spend a 'Mind-Boggling' 9 Hours a Day Using Media, Report Says," CNN, November 3, 2015, https://www.cnn.com/2015/11/03/health/teens-tweens-media-screen-use-report/index.html.

3. National Council of Teachers of English (NCTE), "The NCTE Definition of 21st Century Literacies," February 28, 2013, http://www2.ncte.org/statement/21stcentdefinition/.

4. Frank W. Baker, "Visual Literacy," in *Media Literacy in the K–12 Classroom*, 2nd ed., 41–71. (Arlington, VA: International Society for Technology in Education, 2012).

5. Robyn Seglem and Shelbie Witte, "You Gotta See It to Believe It: Teaching Visual Literacy in the English Classroom," *Journal of Adolescent and Adult Literacy*, 3rd ser., 53, no. 3 (November 2009): 216–26.

6. Melissa Gross and Don Latham, "The Peritextual Literacy Framework: Using the Functions of Peritext to Support Critical Thinking," *Library and Information Science Research* 39, no. 2 (2017): 116–23.

7. Tom Bradshaw and Bonnie Nichols, *Reading at Risk: A Survey of Literary Reading in America*, Research Division Report 46 (Washington, DC: National Endowment for the Arts, 2002).

8. Bradshaw and Nichols, *Reading at Risk*, xiii.

9. *Reading on the Rise: A New Chapter in American Literacy* (Washington, DC: National Endowment for the Arts, 2008); Charlotte Alter, "Common Sense Media Report: Kids Reading for Fun Less Than Ever," *Time*, May 12, 2014, www.time.com/94794/common-sense-media-report-never-read/.

10. Kathryn Zickuhr, Lee Rainie, Kristen Purcell, Mary Madden, and Joanna Brenner, "Younger Americans' Reading and Library Habits," *ERIC* (October 23, 2012), https://eric.ed.gov/?id=ED537514.

11. Gross and Latham, "The Peritextual Literacy Framework."

12. American Association of School Librarians (AASL), "Position Statement on the School Librarian's Role in Reading" (Revised September 1, 2010), www.ala.org/aasl/advocacy/resources/statements/reading-role.

13. American Association of School Librarians (AASL), "National School Library Standards," http://standards.aasl.org/school-librarians/.

14. "What Is Media Literacy, and Why Is It Important?," Common Sense Media: News and Media Literacy, https://www.commonsensemedia.org/news-and-media-literacy/what-is-media-literacy-and-why-is-it-important.

15. Shelbie Witte, Melissa Gross, and Don Latham, "Using the Peritextual Literacy Framework with Young Adult Biographies: Introducing Peritextual Functions with Adolescents in Social Studies," in *Adolescent Literature as a Complement to the Content Areas: Social Science and the Humanities*, ed. Paula Greathouse, Joan F. Kaywell, and Brooke Eisenbach, 69–82 (Lanham, MD: Rowman and Littlefield, 2017).

16. Lawrence R. Sipe and Caroline E. McGuire, "Picturebook Endpapers: Resources for Literary and Aesthetic Interpretation," *Children's Literature in Education: An International Quarterly* 37, no. 4 (2006): 291–304, http://repository.upenn.edu/gse_pubs/38.

17. Sipe and McGuire, "Picturebook Endpapers."

18. Sipe and McGuire, "Picturebook Endpapers."

19. Melissa Gross, Don Latham, Jennifer Underhill, and Hyerin Bak, "The Peritext Book Club: Reading to Foster Critical Thinking about STEAM Texts," *School Library Research* 19 (October 28, 2016): 1–17, www.ala.org/aasl/slr.

20. Shelbie D. Witte, Don L. Latham Jr., and Melissa R. Gross, "Mapping 21st Century Skills: Investigating the Curriculum Preparing Teachers and Librarians," *Education for Information* 31, no. 4 (2015): 209–25.

21. Alter, "Common Sense Media Report."

22. Leigh Ann Jones, "The Great Cover Up: Do Kids Judge Books by Their Cover?," *School Library Journal* 53, no. 6 (June 2007): 44–47, www.slj.com/2007/06/collection-development/the-great-cover-up-do-kids-judge-books-by-their-cover/.

23. Neil Gaiman, "Why Our Future Depends on Libraries, Reading and Day-dreaming," *The Guardian*, October 15, 2013, https://www.theguardian.com/books/2013/oct/15/neil-gaiman-future-libraries-reading-daydreaming.

24. Raina Telgemeier, *Drama* (New York: GRAPHIX, 2012); Carla Jablonksi and Leland Purvis, *Victory: Resistance Book 3* (New York: First Second, 2006).

25. Jason Reynolds, *Long Way Down* (New York: Atheneum, 2017).

26. William Golding, *Lord of the Flies* (repr., New York: Penguin, 2012); Mary Shelley, *Frankenstein* (New York: Dover Publications, 1994); Margaret Atwood, *The Handmaid's Tale* (New York: Anchor First Anchor Books Edition, 1998).

# Critiquing, Resisting, and Remixing Promotional Peritextual Elements of Young Adult Fiction

SEAN P. CONNORS AND ERIN DAUGHERTY

IT IS NOT UNCOMMON FOR OTHERWISE WELL-INTENTIONED TEACHERS AND librarians to caution young people against judging a book by its cover. Although this piece of advice is presumably based on a mature reader's understanding of the value (if not the necessity) of experiencing a story or work of art for oneself, it perpetuates a long-held and problematic assumption that a text—defined in this chapter as the main body of a book, film, television show, video game, and so on—is the core kernel of value with which readers (or viewers) ought to be concerned while overlooking its peritext as superfluous packaging. This chapter aims to complicate this assumption. To do so, we adopt what some readers might perceive as a radical stance, arguing that teachers and librarians have not only a professional responsibility to support young people's attending to peritextual elements that surround media they experience but also an ethical obligation to do so.

## Statement of Problem

Like other forms of media, young adult (YA) fiction can reify as well as disrupt dominant narratives about societal constructs such as race, class, age, gender, sexuality, ability, and so on.[1] Even when a work of YA fiction aspires to communicate progressive ideologies, its peritext—the material that surrounds a text (e.g., book covers, endpapers, title page, author biography, etc.)—can do otherwise.[2] To understand how this is the case, one might consider a distinction that Peter Hollindale makes between surface ideology and passive ideology.[3] As Hollindale defines it, surface ideology refers to an author's personal beliefs and values as they are communicated directly to readers through explicit ideological statements that a narrator or character in a story makes.[4] Passive ideology, on the other hand, is communicated indirectly through an author's unexamined assumptions, with the result that readers can examine a text for the purpose of understanding how it reproduces or resists dominant narratives about social constructs such as femininity, masculinity, race, ability, and so on. In regard to passive ideology, Hollindale states, "A large part of any book is written not by its author but by the world its author lives in."[5] Amending this assertion to account for the role that peritextual elements play in communicating passive ideology, one might note that a portion of any book is written not only by its author but by those who contribute to its material production, including (but not limited to) editors, graphic designers, and other people who help package and market books for consumption by readers. For this reason, peritextual elements always already have the potential to communicate ideologies that may or may not align with those communicated in a text.

This chapter is concerned with the role that promotional peritextual elements, which "interface between a text and its potential audience" and "help to market the work, in terms of making it appealing or providing information that will increase the appeal of the work for its intended user,"[6] play in reproducing and resisting dominant narratives. More specifically, the chapter is concerned with the covers of YA fiction because this genre is popular with young readers and is one that many teachers and librarians work with. In the remainder of this chapter, the concept of promotional peritext is introduced, after which an argument is made for the value of asking young people to examine this category of peritext through the lens of critical literacy. The discussion next turns to an instructional activity that is intended to support young people's critical thinking and critical literacy. To accomplish this, the activity asks students to put the front and back covers of YA novels they read in conversation with their respective narratives to assess how the two align ideologically. Students then redesign the texts' covers for the purpose of either highlighting points of disconnect between the two or critiquing dominant narratives that either the cover or text communicates. To conclude, a rationale is provided for why we regard involving young people in the work of investigating the promotional peritext of YA fiction as an ethical imperative for teachers and librarians.

## Theoretical Framework

In this section, we make a case for educators' inviting students to examine one example of promotional peritext—YA book covers—through a lens of critical literacy. Having introduced and defined the concept of promotional peritext, we next identify four dimensions of critical literacy, an approach to reading that (in part) entails attending closely to texts, defined broadly, for the purpose of determining how they reproduce or resist problematic narratives about people based on their race, gender, social class, and so on.

## Why Should Readers Attend to Promotional Peritext?

In "Introduction to the Paratext," Gérard Genette defines paratext as consisting of peritext—that is, all the elements that surround a text (e.g., front and back covers, copyright information, endpapers, etc.)—and epitext—elements that exist at a remove from a text (e.g., book reviews, advertisements and promotional materials, author interviews, etc.) but which have the potential to shape how readers interpret and understand the text.[7] This chapter is concerned with what Melissa Gross and Don Latham, in presenting their Peritextual Literary Framework (PLF), classify as promotional peritextual elements, one example of which is book covers.[8] In working with young people, teachers and librarians may not always attend to the latter peritextual element closely, but Genette characterizes book covers as establishing a zone of transaction between a text and a reader, the result of which can shape how the text is read.[9] His argument is reminiscent of Louise Rosenblatt's theory of transactional reading, which regards meaning as arising from a transaction between a reader and the design of a text wherein the former draws on her background knowledge and experiences to imbue the latter with meaning.[10] To illustrate this characterization, Genette asks a deceivingly simple question: "Reduced to its text alone and without the help of any instruction for use, how would we read Joyce's *Ulysses* if it were not called *Ulysses*?"[11]

Gross and Latham note that Genette considered functionality the single most important aspect of his theory of peritext.[12] Indeed, they quote him as having argued, "Whatever aesthetic intention may come into play as well, the main issue for the paratext is not to 'look nice' around the text but rather to ensure for the text a destiny consistent with the author's purpose."[13] If the ideological dimension of promotional peritext is shaped not only by an author, however, but also by those who contribute to a book's design and packaging, then the latter half of Genette's assertion is problematic. Indeed, the potential always already exists for the visual (cover art) and linguistic design (plot synopses, review blurbs) of a text's covers to subvert an author's purpose by introducing meanings that conflict with those communicated in a text. Consider, for example, YA novels that feature strong female protagonists who perform a nontraditional version of femininity but who are nonetheless positioned by the book's cover art in traditionally feminine ways.

Similarly, Philip Nel examines how whitewashed covers of YA novels can communicate racial meanings that conflict with those communicated in a text, thereby circumventing an author's purpose.[14] Speaking to the role that YA fiction plays in sustaining structural racism, Nel describes Kate Hart's 2011 examination of over six hundred YA book covers. According to Nel, Hart found that "90 percent featured a White character, 10 percent a character of ambiguous race or ethnicity, 1.4 percent a Latino/a character, 1.4 percent an Asian character, and 1.2 percent a Black character."[15] Still more disturbing, Nel explains that these figures "do not add up to 100 percent because Hart tallied by cover, rather than by cover model—and a cover can have more than one cover model."[16] This is only one example of how the promotional peritext surrounding YA literature fails to acknowledge the diverse students with whom teachers and librarians work daily. Recognizing this failure, teachers and librarians interested in challenging young people to interrogate dominant narratives about race, ethnicity, gender, and so on in works of YA fiction might also invite them to examine a text's promotional peritextual elements critically.

## Examining Promotional Peritextual Elements through the Lens of Critical Literacy

Ernest Morrell defines critical literacy as "the ability not only to read and write, but also to assess texts in order to understand the relationships between power and domination that underlie and inform those texts."[17] He identifies popular culture as an opportunity for educators and students to examine dominant narratives with an eye toward envisioning a more just, more equitable society.[18] Although critical literacy incorporates skills and practices that are associated with critical thinking (for example, analysis and evaluation), Cara Mulcahy argues that the two differ in the emphasis they place on sociopolitical issues and on combining reflection with action to transform society.[19] She thus concludes that "while critical thinking is crucially important in supplying students with the skills to analyze arguments and ideas presented to them in their texts, critical literacy challenges students to identify issues such as gender bias, cultural bias, omissions of narratives by marginalized groups from texts, and to re-write the text to represent a more complete picture."[20]

Mulcahy's discussion of critical literacy draws heavily on the work of Mitzi Lewison, Amy Seely Flint, and Katie Van Sluys, who, having reviewed definitions of the term found in scholarly and professional journals over a period of thirty years, argue that critical literacy has four dimensions.[21] First, critical literacy involves "disrupting the commonplace," which according to Lewison and her colleagues involves learning to see taken-for-granted aspects of everyday life anew.[22] Second, critical literacy entails "interrogating multiple viewpoints," or learning to read texts from perspectives other than one's own.[23] At the same time, it also involves an ability to recognize whose voices are heard and whose are marginalized in or excluded from a text. For Lewison and her colleagues, a third dimension of critical literacy is its concern for sociopolitical issues and the role that texts play in reproducing and resisting dominant discourses and power relationships. Finally, the authors argue that a fourth dimension of critical literacy involves people's acting to redress social justice issues in their communities.

Given the lack of diversity in contemporary YA fiction, there is value in asking young readers to examine elements of promotional peritext through the lens of critical literacy. Sean Connors, for example, describes a class project that asked preservice teachers in a YA literature class to visit a bookstore or library and observe the covers of YA dystopian novels for the purpose of identifying patterns in their visual and linguistic design.[24] Among other things, students were asked to attend to who appeared on the covers of books they examined and who was marginalized or absent; how the language used in plot synopses and review blurbs positioned characters as particular kinds of people with particular interests, concerns, and values; and, finally, what strategies publishers seemingly used to market books to male and female readers. To make these distinctions, students first had to disrupt the commonplace by attending to book covers in a new way while also considering how other people might view them. Additionally, students were asked to consider what their findings suggested about how publishers imagine the audience for YA dystopian fiction, which necessitated their attending to sociopolitical issues.

According to Connors, completing the project helped students appreciate the role that YA book covers play in normalizing whiteness, heteronormativity, and hegemonic masculinity and femininity.[25] To conclude the project, students designed notecards in which they highlighted a social justice issue that their investigation of YA book covers had raised for them. They then returned to the site where they had conducted their observation and left their notecards in a book for another reader to find as a way of raising that person's consciousness about the issue (figure 5.1). In exercising their voices in this way, students were positioned as activists. As a variation of this project, teachers or librarians can ask young readers to put the text of YA novels they have read in conversation

**FIGURE 5.1**

**Sample notecard inserted in a YA dystopian novel**

with the novels' promotional peritextual elements to assess the extent to which the two align ideologically.

## Context

The authors of this chapter are a university professor (Connors) and a graduate student (Daugherty). As literary critics and as readers, we share a common interest in YA fiction, and our work together on various research and teaching projects has allowed us to share ideas about how, as educators, we can support students' attending closely to texts through a lens of critical literacy. Connors regularly teaches courses on YA literature, and the project that we examine in this chapter is one that he has implemented with undergraduate students.

## Putting Critical Literacy to Work by Remixing the Covers of YA Novels

In attending closely to the promotional peritext of a YA novel they have read, readers can ask a variety of critical and analytical questions designed to disrupt the commonplace. For example, in examining artwork on the front or back covers of a novel, one could ask what a graphic designer elected to show and why he might have been motivated to do so. If people appear on a book's covers, one could ask who is represented, who occupies a place in the foreground, and, alternatively, who is backgrounded or missing altogether. A reader could ask how people on the covers of a YA novel are positioned relative to the viewer; for example, do they face the viewer and meet her gaze? Are they depicted from the side? Do they appear in silhouette? Relatedly, what do these choices potentially signify? Readers could ask how people are depicted on the covers of a book, what this depiction potentially suggests about them, and whether the representation perpetuates or resists common stereotypes. Attending to a plot synopsis on the back cover or inside dust jacket fold, one could ask how language is used to position characters in a story as specific kinds of people with particular interests, values, and concerns. On a related note, one could ask which elements of a story a plot synopsis emphasizes, and which it downplays or ignores. Similar questions can be asked of review blurbs, which frequently make intertextual connections by comparing one text to another (e.g., "A romance unlike any seen since _____"). Readers can question what purpose these connections serve and which elements of a story they emphasize. Note that all of these questions involve one's examining a text's covers from multiple perspectives because they necessitate considering how people unlike oneself might perceive them. Throughout this process, readers should put their findings in conversation with their critical analysis of a novel to assess the extent to which the two align ideologically. This approach entails considering whether elements of a text's covers communicate meanings that parallel or conflict with meanings communicated in a story itself.

To provide an opportunity for young people to apply the knowledge their investigation of promotional peritext produces, teachers or librarians can ask students to remix, or redesign, the covers of a YA novel that they have read for the purpose of highlighting an ideological disconnect between the covers and the text. Alternatively, students could use their redesigned covers to comment on a dominant narrative they recognize the original covers or text as communicating. In either case, students should work with all the elements one would expect to find on a text's covers, including a title, author name, cover art, plot synopsis (either on a back cover or inside dust jacket fold), review blurbs, award stickers, and so on. Students are free to determine how they assemble their book covers and what materials they use to do so, provided they incorporate the aforementioned elements in their remixed covers' visual and linguistic designs. Once students finish remixing their covers, they can share their work as part of a class gallery walk, at which time they can ask questions and comment on each other's work. To help students crystallize their learning, teachers or librarians can ask them to present their work to their peers or compose a short essay in which they outline their vision for their redesigned covers and provide a rationale for specific design choices they made to render their critique.

## Application of Idea or Approach

To understand the shape the aforementioned instructional activity might take and to appreciate its potential to support critical and analytical thinking, one might consider a redesigned book cover created by Alex (a pseudonym), a preservice teacher in a young adult literature course. Alex's remixed cover constitutes a response to conflicting gender meanings she recognized in the cover of a movie tie-in edition of *Catching Fire* and in the story itself.[26] The original book cover, shown in figure 5.2, features the white actress Jennifer Lawrence in the

**FIGURE 5.2**

**Front cover of movie tie-in edition of *Catching Fire***

role of Katniss Everdeen, a biracial character, standing alone atop a rock outcropping. The character is dressed in an outfit fans of the series will recognize—hunting boots and a leather jacket—and she wields her iconic bow and arrow. In the context of the story, these items are often interpreted as signifying Katniss's masculine qualities and, hence, as offering female readers another way of performing femininity. In the background, gathering clouds behind the character create the impression that she has wings, an acknowledgment of her status as the Mockingjay, a symbol of resistance throughout the dystopian series. That Katniss appears alone on the cover of the book might be understood to reflect her social positioning in the story as a marginalized figure who rises up to challenge an oppressive government known as the Capitol. In the novel, the character hunts, provides for her mother and sister, elects not to shave her body hair, and demonstrates little interest in romantic relationships. With this in mind, the front cover's visual design could also be interpreted as signifying Katniss's status as a strong, independent female who embodies qualities that some literary critics have associated with girl power.[27]

Alex's redesigned covers, shown in figure 5.3, respond to the cover of *Catching Fire* just discussed by highlighting a conflicting set of gender meanings that her analysis of the novel led her to recognize. Specifically, she sought to critique "the problematic, dominating patriarchal ideology held by the Capitol" that she regarded as contributing to Katniss's regendering over the course of the story. Alex's close reading of *Catching Fire* imagines Katniss not as an independent figure but as a pawn in a game played by the novel's more powerful male characters. Thus, although Alex chose to retain an emphasis on the character in her redesigned cover, she elected to position Katniss as the object of a male gaze. For this reason, the character is shown surrounded by the novel's male characters, including (from right to left, clockwise) Cinna, her personal designer; Haymitch, her trainer for the Hunger Games; President Snow, the totalitarian leader

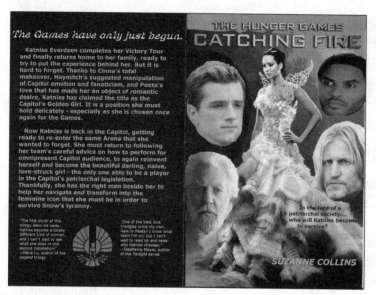

FIGURE 5.3
Student redesigned cover for *Catching Fire*

of Panem; and Peeta, Katniss's fellow tribute from District 12 and a potential love interest in the series. As Alex suggests, each of these characters helps to reposition Katniss as a traditionally feminine figure in the novel. Cinna, for example, emphasizes Katniss's beauty through makeovers and fashion choices; Haymitch pressures her to perform in traditionally feminine ways to win the support of the Capitol audience; Peeta positions her as a love-struck girl, the result of which advantages her in the Games but also renders her "less of a threat to the Capitol's dominating power"; and Snow represents "the enforcer of the Capitol's patriarchal ideology" who insists that Katniss play up her relationship with Peeta when the two embark on their Victor's Tour.

As opposed to her behavior in District 12, once Katniss arrives in the Capitol, she performs gender in a way that aligns more closely with a dominant narrative of traditional femininity. To emphasize this point, in redesigning her cover, Alex elected to alter Katniss's wardrobe, replacing her familiar hunting outfit with a wedding dress that she is made to model for the Capitol audience after her carefully orchestrated engagement to Peeta is announced. Providing a rationale for this design choice, Alex explained that, although "the most common mental conception of Katniss is arguably with her bow and arrow," Alex's decision to depict the character in "her wedding dress combined with her downward gaze" was designed to signify Katniss's status as "a passive, love-struck victor—one that represents traditional femininity in the face of the patriarchy surrounding her." In the context of Alex's redesigned cover, Katniss "does not show any spark of Mockingjay rebellion or more traditionally masculine skills, such as hunting and shooting." Instead, "she has become what the Capitol requires her to be in order to survive their Games," which is conventionally feminine. This point is further emphasized by a question that Alex asks in the lower right-hand corner of her remixed cover: "In the face of a patriarchal society. . . . who will Katniss become to survive?"

The linguistic design of Alex's remixed back cover extends this ideological critique. Rather than emphasize Katniss's stature as a Victor in the Hunger Games, which is the case at the conclusion of the first book in the series, Alex's plot synopsis focuses on the character's gender identity, declaring, "Thanks to Cinna's total makeover, Haymitch's suggested manipulation of Capitol emotion and fanaticism, and Peeta's love that has made her an object of romantic desire, Katniss has claimed the title as the Capitol's Golden Girl." The plot synopsis goes on to highlight the character's return to the Capitol in the second novel, where she must once again "reinvent herself and become the beautiful darling, naive, love-struck girl." To further emphasize the role males play in regendering Katniss, Alex's redesigned plot synopsis sardonically comments, "Thankfully, she has the right men beside her to help her navigate and transform into the feminine icon that she must be in order to survive Snow's tyranny." Even the review blurbs featured near the bottom of the back cover contribute to Alex's critique of the ideological disconnect she recognized between the movie tie-in cover of *Catching Fire* and her critical reading of the novel. In the novel, Katniss is anything but alone; instead, she is positioned in a love triangle with two male characters, Peeta and Gale. Thus, in a review facetiously attributed to Stephenie Meyer, the author of the Twilight series, which has itself been criticized for reproducing dominant narratives about gender in part through its portrayal of a love triangle, Alex emphasizes the novel's romantic angle over its concern with politics. To do so, she has the mock reviewer unabashedly state, "One of the best love triangles since my own."

## Conclusion

Inviting young readers to attend to the ideological dimension of promotional peritext creates opportunities for them to practice the sort of critical thinking skills that many teachers and librarians hope to cultivate. Additionally, such attention to ideology supports students' practicing close reading, a skill that is often emphasized in state standards and which is understood to contribute to students' preparation for college and life beyond. As an added benefit, supporting students' analyzing the visual and linguistic designs of book covers can cultivate their appreciation for the meaning-making potential of resources beyond language, which is too often the sole focus of attention in school. In examining promotional peritext, one can ask what purposes elements such as images, color, and font styles serve, and how they enter into spatial arrangements with language-oriented peritextual elements such as plot synopses and review blurbs to collaboratively communicate meanings that no single element could convey alone. As students gain experience doing this examination, they can experiment with analyzing the semiotic design of other texts that incorporate multiple meaning-making resources. In this sense, inviting young readers to attend to promotional peritext is consistent with many of the professional responsibilities that teachers and librarians are already expected to address.

At a time when public schools are characterized by considerable student diversity, however, it is perhaps not too much to suggest that teachers and librarians also have an ethical obligation to call young people's attention to the promotional peritext that surrounds media they experience. As Connors's students discovered, the covers of YA novels also normalize heterosexuality and traditional gender identities.[28] Strikingly, these students reported having become aware of the role the promotional peritext that surrounds YA fiction plays in reproducing these dominant narratives only after they had been asked to attend to it closely. By encouraging young people to attend critically to promotional peritext, teachers and librarians challenge them to disrupt the commonplace. By creating opportunities for young people to speak over dominant narratives that privilege some groups of people and oppress others, however, teachers and librarians acknowledge students' agency and their capacity to work for a more just, more inclusive world.

## NOTES

1. Sean P. Connors and Ryan Rish, "Troubling Ideologies: Creating Opportunities for Students to Interrogate Cultural Models in YA Literature," *ALAN Review* 42, no. 3 (2015): 22–34.

2. Gérard Genette, "Introduction to the Paratext," *New Literary History* 22, no. 2 (1991): 261–72.

3. Peter Hollindale, "Ideology and the Children's Book," *Signal* 55 (1988): 3–22.

4. Hollindale, "Ideology and the Children's Book," 10–11.

5. Hollindale, "Ideology and the Children's Book," 12, 15.

6. Melissa Gross and Don Latham, "The Peritextual Literacy Framework: Using the Functions of Peritext to Support Critical Thinking," *Library and Information Science Research* 39, no. 2 (2017): 119.

7. Genette, "Introduction to the Paratext."

8. Gross and Latham, "The Peritextual Literacy Framework."

9. Miriam Martinez, Catherine Stier, and Lori Falcon, "Judging a Book by Its Cover: An Investigation of Peritextual Features in Caldecott Award Books," *Children's Literature in Education* 47, no. 3 (2016): 225–41; Genette, "Introduction to the Paratext," 261.

10. Louise M. Rosenblatt, *The Reader, the Text, the Poem: The Transactional Theory of the Literary Work* (Carbondale: Southern Illinois University Press, 1978).

11. Genette, "Introduction to the Paratext," 262.

12. Gross and Latham, "The Peritextual Literacy Framework."

13. Gross and Latham, "The Peritextual Literacy Framework," 116 (emphasis added).

14. Philip Nel, *Was the Cat in the Hat Black? The Hidden Racism of Children's Literature* (New York: Oxford University Press, 2017).

15. Nel, *Was the Cat*, 142.

16. Nel, *Was the Cat*, 142 (emphasis in original).

17. Ernest Morrell, "Toward a Critical Pedagogy of Popular Culture: Literacy Development Among Urban Youth," *Journal of Adolescent and Adult Literacy* 46, no. 1 (2002): 73.

18. Morrell, "Toward a Critical Pedagogy," 72.

19. Cara M. Mulcahy, "The Tangled Web We Weave: Critical Literacy and Critical Thinking," in *Critical Literacy as Resistance: Teaching for Social Justice Across the Secondary Curriculum*, ed. Laraine Wallowitz (New York: Peter Lang, 2008), 15–27.

20. Mulcahy, "The Tangled Web," 26.

21. Mulcahy, "The Tangled Web," 26; Mitzi Lewison, Amy Seely Flint, and Katie Van Sluys, "Taking on Critical Literacy: The Journey of Newcomers and Novices," *Language Arts* 79, no. 5 (2002): 382–92.

22. Lewison, Flint, and Van Sluys, "Taking on Critical Literacy."

23. Lewison, Flint, and Van Sluys, "Taking on Critical Literacy."

24. Sean P. Connors, "Becoming Mockingjays: Encouraging Student Activism through the Study of YA Dystopia," *ALAN Review* 44, no. 1 (2016): 18–29.

25. Connors, "Becoming Mockingjays."

26. Suzanne Collins, *Catching Fire* (New York: Scholastic, 2013).

27. See, for example, Sonya Sawyer Fritz, "Girl Power and Girl Activism in the Fiction of Suzanne Collins, Scott Westerfeld, and Moira Young," in *Female Rebellion*

*in Young Adult Dystopian Fiction,* ed. Sara K. Day, Miranda A. Green-Barteet, and Amy L. Montz (Burlington, VT: Ashgate, 2014), 17–31.

28.  Connors, "Becoming Mockingjays."

$$6$$

# Navigating Kafka's *The Metamorphosis* Using Visual Peritextual Elements

KATIE RYBAKOVA

THIS CHAPTER DISCUSSES PERITEXTUAL ELEMENTS USED TO HELP LEARNERS analyze existential themes within Franz Kafka's novella *The Metamorphosis* in an Introduction to Literature course at the college level.[1] In the last and most challenging unit on existential texts, it was necessary to overlay the themes of existentialism across students' personal, professional, and literary lives. By using the various renditions of covers for Kafka's *The Metamorphosis* and supplementing their analysis with a discussion of existentialist artwork, these learners began to explore the ways in which the peritext functioned as a promotional element for the novella, albeit implicitly. By visually analyzing each cover and different visuals representing existential themes, students were able to predict and exemplify possible existential themes in the novella before even beginning the text. This understanding aided their comprehension of the complex text during reading. The use of visuals speaks to the need to "read" images in the twenty-first century, a skill Robyn Seglem and Shelbie Witte identified as an important complex thinking skill.[2] Reading images also attends to what Charles Kivunja outlined as media literacy.[3]

The goal of this chapter is to share one strategy of using promotional peritextual elements to teach. Although the example in the application section of the chapter outlines the ways in which this strategy was structured in a college-level classroom, it is easily adapted to the high school level as well as for upper-division college classes focused on textual analysis. Ultimately, this narrative serves as a call for a variety of media-rich supplemental material to be used in the literature classroom in addition to the novels we read to help students comprehend, analyze, and find relevance in texts. Furthermore, it is a call to continue exploring what it means to use peritext as a teacher at both the secondary and college levels.

## Statement of Problem

Educators recognize the necessity to attend to their students' needs. This broad statement, when applied to English instructors at both the high school and college levels, means that the texts that students read are relevant, engaging, and accessible, that instruction is facilitated in a way that is clear yet challenging, and that students have the ability to add their opinions and voice to a dialogue, practicing both academic content application and scholarly discourse. When presented with a text that is challenging to read in addition to the task of attending to the text in a way that investigates how complex philosophies such as existentialism are exemplified in the text, students need scaffolds to be able to analyze the text and then make text-to-text connections.[4] In this case, the goal was to analyze *The Metamorphosis* by Kafka and then make text-to-text connections with existential theory. In order to engage in academic discourse of this kind, particularly in the context of working with first-generation college students and other students who do not identify themselves as readers, the use of visual peritext and other visual scaffolds helps set the foundation for productive and in-depth discussions. Analyzing promotional peritext can act as a scaffold to guide not only pre-reading but also during- and post-reading instruction. Specifically, the different cover art available for *The Metamorphosis* allows readers to "begin to think critically about the text based on these peritextual elements."[5]

## Review of Relevant Literature

Gérard Genette, the seminal author regarding paratext, defined the concept as a combination of peritext, or the peripheral components of a book, and epitext, the elements outside a book.[6] Peritextual elements include the cover of the text, the table of contents, and the source notes, among other elements that make up a text aside from the text material itself. Using the Peritextual Literacy Framework (PLF) developed as an extension of Genette's initial theory, Shelbie Witte, Melissa Gross, and Don Latham considered how peritext can serve as a combination of production, promotional, intratextual, navigational, supplemental, and documentary elements.[7] Particularly important to the context of this study, a text's cover could be considered what the researchers identified as promotional peritext, which acts as an "interface between the work and potential readers" and is one of the elements "important to consider in the pre-reading stage if they are present."[8] Identifying and analyzing promotional peritext such as a text cover allow students to determine potential themes and can act as a motivational component in a pre-reading strategy aimed at engaging students to read the text. Witte, Gross, and Latham considered promotional peritext as a way to engage users and stated that the PLF can "function as an aid for media analysis and as a scaffold for teaching critical thinking."[9] To exemplify this strategy in practice, Witte, Gross, and Latham considered how an instructor might help readers unpack the reasons for having two or more different versions of a cover—a specific approach used in this research.[10]

## Context

The class examples and data shared in this chapter were collected over the course of a spring college semester from a rural northeastern college. Over half of the students who attend the college are first-generation college students, defined as those whose parents did not graduate from college.[11] The data were collected from an Introduction to Literature course and included interviews, class observational notes, and all assignments the students turned in. Due to space constrictions, segments of observational notes and interviews will be shared in this narrative. Out of nineteen students, seventeen did not identify themselves as readers during the first week's pretest. Of the nineteen students, ten chose to participate in the interviews, and eight were ultimately interviewed (the two who did not complete interviews after signing informed consent could not make interview appointments due to personal emergencies and were not able to reschedule). Participants included four males and four females. Six of the eight were classified as first-generation college students. The participants majored in a variety of content areas, including business management, elementary education, secondary English education, criminal justice, security and cyber defense, and sports management. All but one were traditional college age. For the purposes of privacy, participants are referred to by pseudonyms: Murphy, Larry, Connor, Sandra, Alexandra, Kasey, John, and Rebecca. The participants are listed in the accompanying text box according to their classifications.

| Participant | Major | First generation | Traditional college age |
|---|---|---|---|
| Murphy | Business Management | Yes | No |
| Larry | Secondary English Education | Yes | Yes |
| Connor | Security and Cyber Defense | Yes | Yes |
| Sandra | Secondary English Education | No | Yes |
| Alexandra | Elementary Education | Yes | Yes |
| Kasey | Elementary Education | No | Yes |
| John | Sports Management | Yes | Yes |
| Rebecca | Criminal Justice | Yes | Yes |

*Subjectivities of the Researcher.* It is essential to identify my subjectivities as the researcher prior to sharing results and narratives based on results. Because I was also the participants' instructor, there is a level of bias that may have impacted the results because students who participated in the study knew me as the instructor of the course. Although I reiterated that participants' grades would not be impacted whether or not they participated in the study, this potential may have impacted the results. I attend to the results as someone who identifies with the social constructivist paradigm and who believes in the effectiveness of using young adult literature as a scaffold in the classroom.[12] These subjectivities may be viewed as limitations or as additional information when reading the results and application.

## Application of Approach

The module on existentialism and existential texts began in the last month of the semester and included a variety of activities, such as a jigsaw on literary periods (a class activity in which students are assigned a particular literary period to investigate in pairs and then rotate through the rest of the pairs to disseminate information and learn about other literary periods) and a Socratic Circle (a class discussion–based activity in which students sit in a circle and discuss the text in an academic way) about the first existential texts of the module—*Looking for Alaska* and *The Call of the Wild*.[13] The module attended to specific objectives in the course syllabus, including "identify elements of style and structure that contribute to the artistry of poetry, drama, and fiction," "identify the characteristics of literature from different periods and cultures," and "write and speak with insight and clarity about literary ideas and forms." *The Metamorphosis* was chosen as a text because it is one of the clearest examples of existential texts and because it is canonical in nature. The course was made up of a purposeful mix of contemporary and canonical texts and used Teri Lesesne's reading ladder design to scaffold up to more complex canonical texts.[14] Furthermore, the goal of the unit was to analyze existential texts to identify the different ways in which existential tropes were symbolized in the texts and the interpretations surrounding them.

In order to further scaffold and identify the ideas of existentialism, such as absurdity, alienation, and Jean-Paul Sartre's idea that "existence precedes essence,"[15] prior to reading and teasing out these concepts in *The Metamorphosis*, students were asked to identify these concepts and discuss the various cover art associated with the novella. Before the lesson in which students visually interpreted different peritextual elements, students engaged in direct instruction about existentialism as well as a jigsaw during which in pairs they defined and identified common tropes in different literary periods.

During the peritextual analysis lesson, students were asked, in a Socratic Circle style, to discuss the similarities and differences among the cover art pictured in figures 6.1, 6.2, and 6.3 and then identify how these images may exemplify existential themes. I purposefully sat back taking notes, seldom facilitating throughout the discussion to allow students to investigate their own ideas further by asking prompting questions of one another. This kind of "hands-off" instruction was gradual and took several months of practice with heavier facil-

**FIGURE 6.1**
*The Metamorphosis*
book cover 1

**FIGURE 6.2**
*The Metamorphosis*
book cover 2

**FIGURE 6.3**
*The Metamorphosis*
book cover 3

itation. Furthermore, students were asked to predict what *The Metamorphosis* was about. The students were given a packet of images and were able to flip back and forth between the cover art images to identify similarities and differences as well as visual existential elements.

These peritextual elements (in the form of cover art) produced different reactions from the students. None of the students had read *The Metamorphosis* before, so their predictions about the text content ranged from "a guy getting eaten by a bug" (Larry) to a more accurate prediction of "a man who feels like he is a bug to the world" (Sandra). Connor suggested that the class not "judge a bug by its cover"; this comment prompted laughter, but then Connor further articulated this observation as a true sentiment: "Well, maybe that's what the book is about. Maybe it's about not judging people for what they look like or what they do for a living." These interpretations showcase critical thinking in that the students were able to connect the visual elements as well as the title of the novella and make predictions (some of them very accurate) about the text—an essential skill of effective readers.[16]

Figure 6.1 was on the first page of the handout and, though initially producing a chorus of "Gross!" from the class, was further acknowledged as a "mask" on a bug that depicted "dark and depressing" themes (Sandra). Alexandra observed that the mask or face had tears, and John was the first to connect this observation to existentialist themes of "absurdity, because a face on a bug doesn't exist in real life—or does it?"

Figure 6.2, which is a fan-created cover, prompted more conversation, as students considered why the man was seemingly naked and why it looked like there were specks of blood outside the cage. Sandra connected the cage and blood to death in a metaphorical sense ("death of identity"), connecting these visual elements to the existential trope of "existence precedes essence," or "nature precedes being." Looking at figure 6.3, students began to make connections of absurdity and death across all three peritexts, considering how a bug and a human might be related if "a human is treated like he is nothing or even disgusting, like a roach" (Murphy).

After predictive work and analysis of the three different covers of *The Metamorphosis*, the class analyzed several pieces of artwork considered to be existential to further their discussion of existential visual elements. One of these images is depicted in figure 6.4.

Larry commented, "It's definitely absurd. It looks like someone dropped a lollipop on the ground and it got covered with crap." Although this literal interpretation of the image was initially what many students agreed upon (other interpretations included "a black city that blew up" and "a moon in front of a sun"), the students started to recognize what this image could represent symbolically. Rebecca suggested, "The blue represents how happy the surroundings are, but the fact that the head is black shows inner turmoil or something." Further conversation included concepts of absurdity in the sense that this image could depict a human and his different selves or anxiety-inducing imagery that represented inner strug-

**FIGURE 6.4**

*The Blue Phantom* by Alfred Otto Wolfgang Schulze, 1951

gle while trying to "be normal on the outside—look at the light colors right out-side the black" (Murphy). The class then was asked to go back to the covers of *The Metamorphosis*—were there similarities and differences that they could see now? This question prompted further discussion about color—or lack of it—in all three renditions of the novella's cover art, and how this could represent the dark and ominous themes that students predicted in the storyline. They expected the death of the man in the text, along with the death of his identity, and the bug as a metaphor for this particular death—an interpretation close in accuracy to the common interpretations of the novella.

## Perceptions of Instructional Approach and Summative Assessment

In addition to my observations and notes of class discussion and the ways in which students were able to connect existentialist themes to *The Metamorphosis* to spark critical thinking about the text, there was evidence through the inter-view data that these strategies were successful in engaging students with the canon and with text analysis as students moved forward in reading *The Meta-morphosis*. Alexandra shared her new interest in canonical texts: "You know, a lot of your lessons are really thought-provoking and engaging, and I feel like I'm actually trying harder than other classes. . . . I feel like I've just been read-ing books that weren't in the canon. Or, I don't know, books that just weren't that interesting to me . . . but these ones are." This quote can connect back to the initial lesson of visual peritextual analysis as a pre-reading strategy. Notice that Alexandra mentioned "thought-provoking" lessons and how she felt more engaged in the reading. This perception can be traced back to the pre-reading scaffold of having students predict what Kafka's text was about, and, by doing so, it allowed students like Alexandra to feel more confident and, thus, willing to "try harder" when reading the canon.

Larry also mentioned the canon: "I think it's interesting because we almost have this perception of the canon as bad, but in actuality it was these guys who wrote these books that almost looked into the future and saw, how, how, I don't want to say twisted, but how different society is going to be from where they are to where we are now." He also commented on the jigsaw as an effective learning activity: "When we write on those big poster board things [giant sticky notes], it's almost . . . this is going to sound bad, but it's almost like you're forced to learn something, because you have to find something either online or in the text or something like that, and it has to be put on the Post-It. And in order to do that, you almost have to memorize it first, say it first, to recall it. So some of the things we've written stuck with me a little bit, so I guess I've learned that way. It's just an easier way of learning. Like I've said, I have a hard time sitting still for more than five minutes."

Larry's comments point to growth that came out of the scaffold of using peritext in two ways. First, he was able to recognize the universality of themes in the canon because he was prepped to view *The Metamorphosis* through an existentialist lens. By recognizing existentialist tropes in the cover art and how they intersect with common philosophical struggles of 2018—mortality, death, identity, the purpose of existence—Larry was able to make the same connections while reading the text itself. The jigsaw comments were interesting in that they showed how Larry first was able to identify aspects of literary periods, but through the use of the peritext activity, he was then able to apply those aspects—a much more complex thinking skill and task.

Murphy commented on his ability to pick themes out of texts in a different way when asked what he had learned: "Well, um, I guess most obvious is that I read differently now, so when I'm reading a novel or something, I'm able to pick out themes better, and I'm able to, um, connect things and see things I didn't necessarily see. Before, I would read a book, and it was basically entertainment." Murphy's quote demonstrated the different ways in which the students learned how to read, including, I believe, being able to "read" promotional peritext.

These quotes serve as a holistic addition to the data shared in the sense that students felt that they came away with new skills and new perceptions of books and text analysis. It is easy for me, as the instructor of the course, to showcase the skills picked up during the peritextual analysis lesson as successful. These interviews confirmed this realization from the students' viewpoints. Through the jigsaw and peritextual analysis, students were set up for success in reading *The Metamorphosis*.

After the lesson analyzing peritextual elements, students read the novella and then answered the following questions in a Socratic Circle summative assessment:

1. Although Gregor was transformed into a bug/creature, his thoughts stayed the same. What do you have to say about the disconnect between mind and body? Does this happen often? What are the consequences? Is it necessary?
2. What are the pressures in Gregor's life, and how did they impact his turning into a bug?
3. Was this a story that centered on the concepts of magical realism, or was this a hallucination or a daydream? In essence, was this a story that should be taken literally or figuratively?
4. What causes anxiety in literature? What causes anxiety in real life? Is anxiety based on how you perceive your goals in life?

Existentialism is based on the premise that every individual creates and defines her own identity and, thus, her own pathways, goals, and the like. Do society and societal norms help or hinder this process? How do we see this process depicted in literature? Does the canon depict this aspect differently than contemporary literature?

These questions served a dual purpose. First, they allowed for summative assessment to determine whether the students were able to not only define but also apply existentialist themes. Second, they lent themselves to a broader conversation about how these themes and tropes apply to students' daily lives—an important task to accomplish considering that many of the students did not initially (according to a pretest) find real-life relevance in any literature, let alone canonical texts. Students were able to identify specific instances of how Gregor was turned into a cockroach and connect them to existentialist themes. Rebecca asked the interpretive question of whether or not Gregor had had a mental breakdown due to stress and anxiety and was hallucinating throughout the story, and how that possibility might be a way in which existential tropes are visible—what is real, and what is not real? Other students connected existentialism and death in the sense of death of identity and how this might cause an existential crisis. This interpretation was connected quickly to their lives and then brought back to how it connected to Gregor's life. The powerful conversations during this summative assessment showed students' abilities to not only define this literary period but also apply it. This outcome was a far cry from the students' initial reactions at the beginning of the course during syllabus overview when they realized they would be reading five texts. Their growth throughout the semester culminated in their identifying themselves not only as readers but also as readers who are able to interpret texts, both traditional and visual, through multiple critical lenses.

## Questions to Consider

Although this example of the use of peritextual analysis might serve as inspiration for a different or adapted instructional practice, it is essential to ask how peritext was involved in the process of planning the lesson itself. Peritext was used explicitly in the lesson in the sense that different renditions of cover art were analyzed, but the term *peritext* was never used with students. Peritext as a concept remained implicit, a term used only in a way to depict the content of the lesson. Is this the way in which educators should use the PLF? Should peritext become explicit to students as they interpret different depictions of the text, whether it be through promotional peritext, such as the cover art, or other forms? Furthermore, should the Peritextual Literacy Framework live predominantly in the field of information literacy, or should it be used more explicitly in teacher preparation and instructional practice? As with much research, typically the questions generated exceed the questions "answered"; this study is one of those cases. It is important, then, to continue to unpack how peritextual elements could and should be used in instruction, regardless of the level.

## Conclusion

The peritextual analysis lesson in this chapter served as one instructional example of the PLF in action as a way to encourage students' abilities to understand and navigate a complex canonical text. Knowledge of the way peritext can be used to formulate a lesson is essential for instructors in that it promotes critical thinking. Holistically, this lesson provided a venue for cross-disciplinary experiences (e.g., art, philosophy intersections with literature) rich in different forms of text. The students were able to use promotional peritextual elements as a way to inform predictions of the text. Furthermore, they were able to use the interpretation of existential artwork to connect to the different cover renditions of *The Metamorphosis* and exemplify how all four images portray existential themes. This connection helped them analyze the complex text. This process indicates, then, that in practice peritext can aid and support comprehension and appreciation of texts, much as Gross and Latham discuss.[17] It is essential that the use of peritext in practice continues and that instructors and researchers continue to showcase the bridge between theory and practice in their classrooms using the PLF.

## NOTES

1. Franz Kafka, *The Metamorphosis*, trans. Ian Johnston (1999), http://historyworld .org/The_Metamorphosis_T.pdf.

2. Robyn Seglem and Shelbie Witte, "You Gotta See It to Believe It: Teaching Visual Literacy in the English Classroom," *Journal of Adolescent and Adult Literacy*, 3rd ser., 53, no. 3 (November 2009): 216–26.

3. Charles Kivunja, "Do You Want Your Students to Be Job-Ready with 21st Century Skills? Change Pedagogies: A Pedagogical Paradigm Shift from Vygotskian Social Constructivism to Critical Thinking, Problem Solving, and Siemens' Digital Connectivism," *International Journal of Higher Education* 3, no. 3 (2014).

4. Shelbie Witte and Katie Rybakova, "Digging for Deeper Connections: Building Multimodal Text Scaffolds," ALAN Review, 2017; Teri Lesesne, *Reading Ladders: Leading Students from Where They Are to Where We'd Like Them to Be* (Portsmouth, NH: Heinemann, 2010).

5. Melissa Gross and Don Latham, "The Peritextual Literacy Framework: Using the Functions of Peritext to Support Critical Thinking," *Literacy and Information Science Research* 39, no. 2 (2017): 128.

6. Gérard Genette, *Paratexts: Thresholds of Interpretation* (New York: Cambridge University Press, 1997).

7. Shelbie Witte, Melissa Gross, and Don Latham, "Using the Peritextual Literacy Framework with Young Adult Biographies: Introducing Peritextual Functions with Adolescents in Social Studies," in *Adolescent Literature as a Complement to the Content Areas: Social Science and the Humanities*, ed. Paula Greathouse, Joan F. Kaywell, and Brooke Eisenbach, 69–82 (Lanham, MD: Rowman and Littlefield, 2017).

8. Witte, Gross, and Latham, "Using the Peritextual Literacy Framework," 71–72.

9. Witte, Gross, and Latham, "Using the Peritextual Literacy Framework," 117.

10. Witte, Gross, and Latham, "Using the Peritextual Literacy Framework."

11. Janice Wiggins, foreword to *Faculty and First Generation College Students: Bridging the Classroom Gap Together, New Directions for Teaching and Learning* 127 (San Francisco: Jossey-Bass, 2011), 1–4.

12. Lev Vygotski, "The Problem of the Cultural Development of a Child," *Journal of Genetic Psychology* 36, no. 3 (1929): 415–34.

13. John Green, *Looking for Alaska* (New York: Penguin Group, 2005); Jack London, *The Call of the Wild* (New York: Macmillan, 1990).

14. Lesesne, *Reading Ladders*.

15. Jonathan Webber, *The Existentialism of Jean-Paul Sartre, Routledge Studies in Twentieth-Century Philosophy* (New York: Routledge, 2009).

16. Nell Duke and P. David Pearson, "Effective Practices for Developing Reading Comprehension," in *What Research Has to Say about Reading Instruction*, ed. Alan E. Farstrup and S. Jay Samuels (Newark, DE: International Reading Association, 2002), 205–42.

17. Gross and Latham, "The Peritextual Literacy Framework."

# PART III

# PROVIDING CRITICAL THINKING OPPORTUNITIES THROUGH PERITEXTUAL ANALYSIS

*Consumed in the fires on that longest of nights and most terrible of days weren't simply black Tulsa's half dozen hotels, two movie theaters, and more than twenty grocery stores, but entire lifetimes of sweat and toil and hard work.*

—Scott Ellsworth, author of *Death in the Promised Land*[1]

---

*I don't believe that history holds easy answers or simple lessons, because those answers and lessons are stretched out over thousands— millions—of untold stories.*

—Jennifer Latham, in the author's note of *Dreamland Burning*[2]

# A Sense of Time and Place

*Using the Author's Note in a Historical Fiction Novel*

REBECCA WEBER AND KEVIN DYKE

THIS CHAPTER DESCRIBES THE USE OF HISTORICAL FICTION TO HELP STU-
dents establish a connection to history and geography. In this case, the historical
event is the Tulsa Race Riot of 1921, and the text in question is the 2017 novel
*Dreamland Burning* by Jennifer Latham.[3] *Dreamland Burning* is a historical fiction
murder mystery set in Tulsa, Oklahoma, in both the present and 1921. As it
moves between past and present, *Dreamland Burning* addresses issues of race,
racism, and historical memory. The main peritextual element under study is the
author's note. Educators can use the author's note to delve into the historical
events behind the novel as a way to encourage students to critically assess the
idea of history as neutral. The chapter begins by introducing the issue of teaching critical thinking through history. Next, we briefly review the relevant literature concerning author's notes, critical thinking, and the role of objectivity in
history. Then, we provide a summary of the events of the Tulsa Race Riot and the
author's note in *Dreamland Burning*. The chapter ends with example classroom
applications of the author's note and a list of resources for further learning.

Dreamland Burning contrasts the story of Rowan Chase, a 17-year-old who
lives in modern-day Tulsa with her African American mother and Caucasian
father, with that of 17-year-old Will Tillman, who lives in Tulsa during the
summer of 1921 with his Caucasian father and Osage mother. Siblings (and

Greenwood residents) Joseph and Ruby Goodhope also play a major role in Will's story. In both time lines, the characters experience racism, directly and indirectly. Throughout the novel, Latham expertly weaves together the modern and historical elements, encouraging comparison between the events depicted, demonstrating the novel's tagline that "history isn't over yet."

## Statement of Problem

Thinking critically about a topic is essential in today's information landscape. Whether students are looking at current events or historical ones, the ability to examine the motives and ideas behind an issue is crucial. In this chapter, we explore the connections between representations of history and the reality of the historical event by using the author's note accompanying the text of *Dreamland Burning*. Although this text is an example, using peritext, in this case the author's note, to understand historical events portrayed in historical fiction is the broader concept. Looking at the author's note gives the reader a more complete picture of the research and thought that went into creating the story. This exploration of the author's note is applicable not only for the high school or college classroom but for life in general. Students should know how to examine all texts and the arguments within—be they in print or online.

History is complicated, especially when it is controversial. Everyone approaches history through a lens of experience and perspective. Many of Oklahoma's students know little or nothing about the Tulsa Race Riot, though it is now part of the public school curriculum for the state of Oklahoma. The records of the Tulsa Race Riot are incomplete and, in some cases, blatantly edited. In instances such as these, educators and librarians must work to provide the most complete record possible. It is important for readers to broaden their perspective, to look to primary sources for information, and to understand implicit bias. These are skills students need as they wade through a flood of information available to them, particularly when information about the past is more readily accessible through online archives.

## The Author's Note in Historical Fiction

At its best, historical fiction provides a "lived-through experience" that makes the lives of others more accessible.[4] In these works, the author's note serves as a bridge between fact and fiction, highlighting research the author did to ensure historical accuracy and emphasizing issues the author deems important.[5]

Using historical fiction as a teaching tool can accomplish several purposes. It can increase students' interest in a particular historical event such as the Tulsa Race Riot, the Kennedy assassination, or September 11. The Tulsa Race Riot took place before current high school students' grandparents or possibly their great grandparents were born. Although it is easy to read statistics in a textbook and not fully relate them to actual people living so long ago, the use of historical fiction has been shown to positively affect students' development of empathy.[6] In *Dreamland Burning*, Latham describes one of the dead men that Will Tillman encounters the night of the race riot:

> Judging from the swatch of uncharred skin between his shirtsleeve and the burned stump of his right hand, he'd been a Negro once. A length of rope looped round his neck and snaked along behind him. His body was broken, his suit in tatters. Someone had dragged him behind an automobile, though whether or not he'd been much alive when it happened, I chose not to ponder overmuch.[7]

The stark description of death here, even in fiction, makes this event visceral for the reader.

The author's note provides readers a peek into the author's approach to research and the crafting of the story.[8] Further, an author's note may "promote more insightful and thoughtful use of books by teachers (and readers in general) who otherwise lack the personal experiences, knowledge, and comfort level that equip them to present the book in a culturally conscious way."[9] In the example of *Dreamland Burning*, readers witness and empathize with the experience of racism in 1921 and 2017 Tulsa from the perspectives of two biracial teenagers. Being able to explore and understand cultural experiences outside one's own is essential to developing empathy for others and can lead to a deeper understanding of the text.

## Critical Thinking

Today, an emphasis on standardized testing often discards the factors of critical thinking in favor of curriculum focused on test preparation.[10] At the same time, however, many state and national standards do recognize the importance of critical thinking for student success. For example, the American Association of School Librarians (AASL), a division of the American Library Association (ALA), in its Standards Framework, outlines the importance of critical thinking using six domains: inquire, include, collaborate, create, explore, and engage with the information and other people.[11] Similarly, in its curriculum standards for social studies, the National Council for the Social Studies states that students acquire cultural competency "through multiple modes, including fiction and nonfiction, data analysis, meeting and conversing with peoples of divergent backgrounds, and completing research into the complexity of various cultural systems."[12] Additionally, the National Council of Teachers of English argues that literacy in the twenty-first century requires an ability to "pose and solve problems collaboratively and strengthen independent thought, . . . synthesize multiple streams of simultaneous information," and critically analyze multimedia texts.[13] The emphasis on exploring multiple sources is key to helping students develop critical thinking skills. Exposing students to more than one source of information can help students analyze viewpoints, question source materials, and draw their own conclusions. Further, Melissa Gross and Don Latham discuss the importance of peritext as a tool to foster critical thought.[14] The authors suggest that students at all levels can understand the concepts of peritext. They state, "Emergent literacy programming as demonstrated in the literature can include such concepts as author, illustrator, publisher, as well as examining book covers and end papers."[15] Concepts of the book and its parts can be the basis for students' examining texts and diving into further study as they progress in their education. The author's note for *Dreamland Burning* provides students with avenues for analyzing the novel as a literary work and as a tool to use in the interpretation of the historical events depicted.

## Objectivity and Historical Research

Using historical fiction to introduce an event such as the Tulsa Race Riot offers teachers a chance to disrupt the idea of purely objective or "neutral" history. When the American Historical Association was founded in 1884, its practitioners, eager to distinguish themselves from amateurs, placed enormous value on the idea of objectivity in their work. Belief in the scientific method and its applicability to historical investigation reigned supreme. The tradition of objectivity and the impulse to accept past events as static, atomistic facts influenced the rise of "consensus history" in the United States in the period following the Second World War. Consensus historians argued that ideological differences within the United States were minor quibbles, not seismic events such as those that gripped Europe during the same period. As Peter Novick put it, "The consensus among historians in this period is in some ways surprising, for there was never another time in American history in which, overall, there was so little consensus."[16] Viewed through the lens of consensus history, the fifty-year omission of the events of the Tulsa Race Riot from the historical record is comprehensible. Such a nakedly violent expression of racism does not fit within a grand narrative of basic American cooperation and coexistence. Yet, the long absence of the Tulsa Race Riot from the historical record was not simply a result of the dominance of a particular branch of academic history. Rather, several authors suggest that the white leaders of the city of Tulsa, the state of Oklahoma, and local Tulsa newspapers took deliberate action to obfuscate the events of May 31–June 1, 1921.[17] For example, for years black survivors have spoken of an editorial published in the *Tulsa Tribune* explicitly calling for the lynching of Dick Rowland. To date, an intact copy of the city edition of the paper has never been found (the microfilmed version is missing the editorial and front pages).

Confirming or denying the deliberate destruction of evidence is beyond the scope of this chapter. Rather, the events of the Tulsa Race Riot present teachers with a chance to demonstrate to students that archival materials (what historians reverently call the "evidence") are not a neutral source of truth and that what gets archived is a highly contextual process, beginning long before any material gets into the hands of an archivist.[18] The power of historical fiction such as *Dreamland Burning* is that it enables us to escape the tyranny of evidence and to instead introduce and reflect on larger questions. In turn, Latham's author's note provides a direct path to the primary source material through a number of links to Tulsa Race Riot collections at institutions such as the University of Tulsa and the Oklahoma History Center.

## History of the Tulsa Race Riot

Tulsa's early African American residents settled in the northeastern part of the city, with primary business development taking place on Greenwood Avenue. Greenwood prospered and became known as "Black Wall Street."[19] In the span of eighteen hours between May 31 and June 1, 1921, Greenwood burned to the ground during what would later be known as the Tulsa Race Riot. The pretense for the riot was an alleged rape on May 30, when Dick Rowland, a 19-year-old black man, was accused by a 17-year-old white teenage elevator operator named Sarah Page. Prior to Rowland's arrest, the *Tulsa Tribune* published a front-page story with the incendiary headline "Nab Negro for Attacking Girl in Elevator," simultaneously stoking anger among white Tulsans and fear for Rowland's safety among the black residents of Greenwood. An increasingly large crowd of whites gathered outside the county jail.

A group of black residents (among them many veterans of the recently concluded World War) armed themselves and walked to the courthouse, vowing to prevent any harm from coming to Rowland. Whites began to talk of a "Negro invasion" of Tulsa and scrambled to arm themselves, breaking into sporting goods stores and other businesses in search of weaponry (while also helping themselves to cash and other valuables). Back at the courthouse, a white man attempted to forcibly disarm a black man. The gun went off, and with that, "all hell broke loose."[20] The National Guard interned Greenwood's residents in concentration camps, ostensibly for their safety. Meanwhile, a white mob looted and burned the unprotected community.

Reading an account of the Tulsa Race Riot such as this fails to convey the visceral horror of what happened. *Dreamland Burning* not only discusses the events of the riot but also explicitly connects it to present-day issues of racism and police violence. These connections can be used to spur classroom discussion alongside the use of the author's note to drive primary source investigation.

## The Author's Note in *Dreamland Burning*

In *Dreamland Burning*, Latham's note appears at the end of the novel and emphasizes the reality of the Tulsa Race Riot, urging readers to learn more. The note provides an ideal starting point for classroom-based, in-depth investigation, as well as an opening to connect the text with nonfiction elements. Latham writes, "Between the evening of May 31 and the afternoon of June 1, 1921, white rioters looted the thriving African American section of Tulsa known as Greenwood. After taking what they wanted, they burned the rest to the ground. . . . At least 8000 black men, women, and children lost everything they owned."[21] After giving more statistics from the race riot, Latham lets her readers know how she merged fact and fiction, saying, "If you are wondering where fact ends and fiction begins in *Dreamland Burning*, a good guideline is [that] any characters with dialogue are fictional. . . . Speakeasies, brothels, and Jim Crow laws were real."[22] Latham also explains that her use of the term *race riot* was due to its being the most commonly used phrase historically while not denying the perhaps greater precision of other terms such as *race massacre* and *race war*. The inclusion of racial slurs was also purposeful: "These words are ugly, offensive, and hateful, but I chose to include them because I felt that blunting the sharp edges of racism in a book about genocide would be a mistake."[23]

After her explanation of some of the stylistic choices used in the novel, Latham mentions several online resources, including an online exhibit from the Tulsa Historical Society and articles from the *Tulsa World* and the *New York Times*, as good places to begin further research. She goes on to list the sites where she did the extensive research behind the novel. The list functions as a resource and as an acknowledgment of the institutions and individuals who made the writing of *Dreamland Burning* possible.

## Practical Methods and Application of Ideas or Approach

The primary challenge to using historical fiction in the classroom is helping learners recognize and separate fact from fiction. As noted, Latham addresses this problem directly in the author's note for *Dreamland Burning*. In the classroom then, having learners read the author's note before reading the novel itself would do much to ameliorate the issue of distinguishing fact from fiction. Additionally, Rebecca Perini suggests that "attending to such notes can help teachers determine which elements of the book warrant greater attention in order to extend the learning that takes place."[24] Further, readers can reflect on how the author's note influenced their understanding of the novel and the historical context in which it is set. For example, educators might use a writing prompt such as, "How did the author's note influence your understanding or impression of the novel (or the historical event behind the novel)?"[25]

## Conclusion

The Tulsa Race Riot is the defining moment of the city's history. A 2012 law requires its inclusion in Oklahoma's social studies curriculum. In the last twenty years, more has been written about the event than ever before. In spite of all this, many Oklahoma students, even those (perhaps especially those) in Tulsa, barely engage with the riot and its legacy. Scott Ellsworth put it best when he asked, "[S]hall Tulsa be simply the city of the riot, or the city that healed the bitter wounds that it caused? Shall we be the city that merely and begrudgingly acknowledged this tragedy, or the city that did something about it?"[26] These questions are applicable not just for Tulsa itself but also for Oklahoma and beyond. *Dreamland Burning*, a gripping novel written by a resident of Tulsa, offers a way for students to confront the past and make connections to today. Latham's author's note adds another layer to her novel. Here is its final paragraph:

> Like Rowan's mom I don't believe that history holds easy answers or simple lessons, because those answers and lessons are stretched out over thousands—millions—of untold stories. But I do believe that if we seek those stories out, and if we listen to them and talk to each other with open hearts and minds, we can start to heal. I believe that good people working together can create meaningful change. And I believe that the Josephs, Rubys, and Wills of this world are stronger than the Vernon Fishes.[27]

The themes Latham incorporates throughout the novel—of friendship, appreciating others, and learning their stories—she boldly declares in personal and striking language. By placing the author's note at the end of the novel, Latham can unwind facts from fiction but also entwine them again by mentioning Joseph, Ruby, Will, and Vernon Fish, all of whom readers know intimately by the end of the novel. When readers understand the relationships among these four characters, the statement Latham makes to conclude her author's note becomes even more affecting. The note allows readers to see the logic, research, and creativity that make a novel possible. Most important, as with *Dreamland Burning*, an author's note can explicitly detail the author's thoughts about and purpose for the novel.

## NOTES

1. Scott Ellsworth, "'City at the Crossroads' Remarks by Scott Ellsworth," October 29, 2009, https://www.jhfcenter.org/dinner-of-reconciliation.

2. Jennifer Latham, *Dreamland Burning* (New York: Little, Brown, 2017).

3. Latham, *Dreamland Burning*.

4. Cathy Beck, Shari Nelson-Faulkner, and Kathryn Mitchell Pierce, "Talking about Books: Historical Fiction: Teaching Tool or Literary Experience?," *Language Arts* 77, no. 6 (2000): 546–55.

5. Rebecca L. Perini, "The Pearl in the Shell: Author's Notes in Multicultural Children's Literature," *Reading Teacher* 55, no. 5 (2002): 428–31; Suzette Youngs and Frank Serafini, "Comprehension Strategies for Reading Historical Fiction Picturebooks," *Reading Teacher* 65, no. 2 (October 1, 2011): 115–24, https://doi.org/10.1002/TRTR.01014.

6. Linda S. Levstik, "Historical Narrative and the Young Reader," *Theory Into Practice* 28, no. 2 (1989): 114–19; Beck, Nelson-Faulkner, and Pierce, "Talking about Books."

7. Latham, *Dreamland Burning*, 295.

8. Beck, Nelson-Faulkner, and Pierce, "Talking about Books."

9. Perini, "The Pearl in the Shell," 428.

10. Kenneth E. Vogler and David Virtue, "'Just the Facts, Ma'am': Teaching Social Studies in the Era of Standards and High-Stakes Testing," *Social Studies* 98, no. 2 (March 1, 2007): 54–58, https://doi.org/10.3200/TSSS.98.2.54-58.

11. American Association of School Librarians, "AASL Standards Framework for Learners," 2018, http://standards.aasl.org/wp-content/uploads/2017/11/AASL-Standards-Framework-for-Learners-pamphlet.pdf.

12. National Council for the Social Studies, "National Curriculum Standards for Social Studies: A Framework for Teaching, Learning, and Assessment," National Council for the Social Studies, 2010, https://www.socialstudies.org/standards.

13. National Council of Teachers of English, "The NCTE Definition of 21st Century Literacies," 2013, http://www2.ncte.org/statement/21stcentdefinition.

14. Melissa Gross and Don Latham, "The Peritextual Literacy Framework: Using the Functions of Peritext to Support Critical Thinking," *Library and Information Science Research* 39, no. 2 (2017): 116–23.

15. Gross and Latham, "The Peritextual Literacy Framework," 121.

16. Peter Novick, *That Noble Dream: The "Objectivity Question" and the American Historical Profession, Ideas in Context* (Cambridge: Cambridge University Press, 1988), 63.

17. James S. Hirsch, *Riot and Remembrance: The Tulsa Race War and Its Legacy* (Boston: Houghton Mifflin, 2002), https://books.google.com/books?hl=en&lr=&id=MnPs7DQpsa8C&oi=fnd&pg=PA1&dq=%22tulsa+race+riot%22&ots=kknq6pbQtr&sig=Q8T152SN3QMAZK-4zd_XUP-eu-4.

18. David Thomas, Simon Fowler, and Valerie Johnson, *The Silence of the Archive, Principles and Practice in Records Management and Archives* (London, UK: Facet Publishing, 2017).

19. Mary E. Parrish, *Race Riot 1921: Events of the Tulsa Disaster, rev. ed.* (Tulsa, OK: Out on a Limb Publishing, 1998).

20. Hirsch, *Riot and Remembrance.*

21. Latham, *Dreamland Burning,* 367.

22. Latham, *Dreamland Burning,* 368.

23. Latham, *Dreamland Burning,* 369.

24. Perini, "The Pearl in the Shell," 431.

25. Gross and Latham, "The Peritextual Literacy Framework."

26. Ellsworth, "'City at the Crossroads' Remarks by Scott Ellsworth."

27. Latham, *Dreamland Burning,* 370–71.

$$8$$

# Discourse about Illustrated Book Dust Jackets in a First-Grade Classroom

LUCIANA C. DE OLIVEIRA, LOREN JONES, AND SHARON L. SMITH

PICTURE BOOKS AND OTHER FORMS OF ILLUSTRATED CHILDREN'S LITERA-
ture have long been recognized as students' entry point into literacy,[1] serving
a myriad of cognitive and aesthetic purposes. Elementary teachers frequently
incorporate illustrated texts beginning in the earliest years of schooling and
typically continue to use them through the upper elementary grades and even
into middle school[2] in order to teach both literacy and content. In addition to
reading books for school, children often seek out different forms of literature
to read for enjoyment.

Although illustrated children's literature is often viewed as a more simplistic
literary form, research has shown that the interaction of images and written
text creates a complex, aesthetic experience that allows students to develop
high-level cognitive skills.[3] When children immerse themselves in multimodal
texts, they can begin to form critical perspectives of the literature they are
reading, applying these points of view to their own lives, their communities,
and the world around them. Because illustrated children's books are the primary texts used in elementary education, the various semiotic modes and
meaning-making elements found in this literature greatly influence students'
literacy learning and their social development.[4]

Illustrated children's books become even more influential and key to literacy instruction as the current educational landscape calls for more sophisticated and complex literacy skills necessary for success in classrooms and participation in society.[5] Not only are these skills pertinent for reading and English language arts, but they are also intertwined throughout and inseparable from core content areas (e.g., mathematics, science, social studies).[6] Even though students are surrounded by literature across content areas, teaching elementary students to make connections and to decipher all the various complex meaning-making elements in this literature is crucial to providing students access to these texts and their content.

## The Picture Book Dust Jacket as a Peritextual Element

The meaning-making elements of a text extend outside the words and pictures found in the story. In fact, elements such as the dust jacket of the book, the table of contents, the endpapers, and the title, copyright, and dedication pages greatly contribute to students' interpretation and comprehension of the story.[7] This chapter focuses on one of these important peritextual elements, the dust jacket. The dust jackets of children's books, commonly referred to as covers by classroom teachers, often contain illustrations and text, such as the title and the author and illustrator names. Dust jackets can also include medals or awards that the book has received and recognitions or endorsements from different organizations or notable individuals or both. Because the book's dust jacket is a student's first entrance into a text, these different components provide readers with important insights into genre, setting, characters, and plot and give them an overall idea of what the story will be like.[8] Even before the book is opened, readers can participate in activities related to the book dust jacket that spark their interest and engagement in the text while providing them opportunities to make connections and predictions about the story they are going to read.

Although researchers agree about the importance and the value of the book dust jacket in children's literature, there is still a dearth of research in this area. Few studies have explored the affordances of the various peritextual elements of texts, and even fewer have focused on the dust jacket of illustrated children's literature.[9] In addition, this important component of books is regularly overlooked or glossed over in elementary classrooms as teachers and students alike rush to begin the story. Unfortunately, educators often model and reinforce this inattention to book dust jackets, doing little more than reading the title of the book and showing the dust jacket when reading aloud to students. A large contributing factor to this lack of attention and time spent on book dust jackets may be that elementary teachers have not been exposed to or taught about the instructional benefits that a careful examination of book dust jackets can provide.[10]

This chapter aims to contribute to this underdeveloped field by exploring how a first-grade teacher used book dust jackets to introduce students to two stories. The next section provides the theoretical framework that served as a foundation for this study, building on previous related research. Following the theoretical framework, the context of the study is outlined. Next, the application of this approach in a first-grade classroom is presented. Though this chapter focuses on first grade, the ideas presented can be used across all levels of education. This chapter concludes with specific strategies for how to focus on a peritextual element, the book dust jacket, and how to use it to enhance literacy instruction.

## Theoretical Framework

This framework draws on research about peritextual elements, literacy, and picture books. Almost all literary works are reinforced and accompanied by different verbal and visual productions that extend and present them.[11] The concept of peritext was defined by Gérard Genette[12] as referring to these peripheral features of texts and was first applied to adult works. Since then, this concept has been applied to a wide variety of media, including picture books and other illustrated children's literature.[13] Children's literature includes many peritextual features that supplement the words and illustrations of the story, such as the dust jacket, the endpapers, the title and dedication pages, and awards and medals.[14] Peritext is especially important with picture books, considering the shortness of the text.[15] The dust jackets of picture books afford children rich meaning-making possibilities and preparation for reading the text.[16] This important "boundary" peritextual element,[17] the dust jacket, presents readers with particular information, including the author's name, the title of the work, and illustrations. The Peritextual Literacy Framework (PLF) developed by Melissa Gross and Don Latham[18] outlines the different functions of peritext and uses it to help readers think critically about the text.[19] This chapter will focus on the dust jackets of two picture books that fulfill the promotional peritextual function.[20] The promotional function of peritext is composed of various elements that serve to interface between the text and its readers, often influencing the reader's view of the text.[21]

## Participants and Setting

This study was conducted in an elementary classroom in a state in the southeastern United States. Ms. Cabana (all names are pseudonyms) is a first-grade teacher at Sunnyside Elementary, a school with a high number of English language learners (ELL students) and bilingual students. Sunnyside serves more than 1,200 students coming from more than fifty countries, and Ms. Cabana's class reflected this diversity. She had twenty-four students in her classroom, with four Level 4 ESOL (English for speakers of other languages) students and twelve bilingual students not labeled ESOL. These students contributed to a classroom climate of rich cultural and linguistic diversity. Ms. Cabana was selected as a participant in this study due to her passion and commitment to advocating for bilingual students. The focus of the larger study on which this chapter is based was on scaffolding language and literacy activities for ELL students and bilingual students.

## Data Collection

The authors are a team composed of a university professor (de Oliveira), a doctoral candidate (Jones), and a second-year doctoral student (Smith). Together, we make up a research team that works closely with Ms. Cabana and other teachers at Sunnyside Elementary. We meet weekly to share and develop ideas, create materials for literacy lessons, debrief, and analyze collected data.

Data from this project were collected in Ms. Cabana's classroom during the 2016–17 school year. These data were taken from a larger project database for a classroom study that focused on the use of planned and interactional scaffolding in the classroom with bilingual students. This full database included field notes of school activities; field notes and audio-recorded observations of classroom instruction; interviews with the teacher; and documents, lesson plans, and photos of classroom displays.

## Application of Idea

The present study focused on instructional data, supported by the larger database. Specifically, data analysis focused on how Ms. Cabana used the dust jackets to introduce two books to students and to connect to students' experiences and backgrounds. This analysis explores the classroom discourse by the teacher and students, when Ms. Cabana introduces the books to students and when the class reads the books and refers to the dust jackets. This exercise was observed within each literacy unit that took place in Ms. Cabana's classroom; however, the excerpts of classroom discourse surrounding these two texts exemplified her use of the dust jackets on the front and back of each book as a promotional peritextual element.

The first book, *Last Stop on Market Street*,[22] is a picture book about a boy named CJ riding the bus with his grandma one Sunday after church. CJ asks several questions that are answered in an inspiring way by Grandma, who helps him appreciate the diverse world around them. The second book, *Dolphins at Daybreak*,[23] is a beginning chapter book that is part of the Magic Tree House series that follows two children, Jack and Annie, as they go on exciting adventures, traveling through time and space in a magic tree house. In this particular text, the children are trying to become "master librarians," which requires them to solve four riddles through exploring marine life and ocean animals in order to collect books for their treehouse. Before reading the books to students, Ms. Cabana explored the dust jackets of the books in specific ways.

The following brief exchange highlights how Ms. Cabana facilitated a meaningful conversation with her students about the dust jacket of *Last Stop on Market Street*. This excerpt comes from a lengthier discussion in which Ms. Cabana prepared students to read their new text by touching on their personal experiences in relation to travel and spending time with family members.

1. *Ms. C:* I want everyone to look at the cover of *Last Stop on Market Street* and I want you to notice all the details you see in this cover. I want you to think, "What is going on in this picture?" Now I want you to turn to someone who is near you and tell them what you think is going on in this picture.
2. *Ms. C:* So Mateus, who was your partner?
3. *Mateus:* Jonas.

4. *Ms. C:* What did Jonas think was going on in this picture?

5. *Mateus:* I don't remember.

6. *Jonas:* Ms. C, how do they make the same covers and the same books?

7. *Ms..C:* Good. So, Jonas, you have a question about printing and books, so we will talk a little bit more about that later. I want you to keep that question in your mind, [and] we will put it on a Post-It note. What Jonas was noticing, and it's good to see this, those little stickers are awards that the books get.

8. *Jonas:* Do all books have them?

9. *Ms. C:* All of these will have them. Now, when I ask you about what is going on in the picture, I am glad that you noticed that this book has a lot of awards, and now I am kinda looking at this section of it, what's happening here? Jonas, what did Mateus notice about the cover?

10. *Mateus:* I told him that I think all the people are going to end up on Market Street.

11. *Ms. C:* Okay, so you think everyone is going to end up on Market Street?

12. *Mateus:* Yea.

13. *Sabrina [student teacher working with Sonia, an ELL student]:* Sonia told me that she thinks that all the people are going to Target on the bus.

14. *Ms. C:* Okay, so Sonia is noticing the transportation that they are using, they are using a bus, and Sonia, do you ride a bus to go to Target? No? You think a lot of people go to Target? What made you say that they are going to Target? What made you think that?

15. *Sonia:* [inaudible]

16. *Ms. C:* It is true that Target usually has a lot of people that come in and out of there, so Target is pretty busy, and this bus looks busy, it looks crowded. Any other ideas? What else do you notice going on in this picture?

17. *Lucy:* He thinks that the little kid and the grandma are gonna come on the bus.

18. *Ms. C:* So now, Lucy is pointing to something else that Jacob thought, and what's really great is that you know your own opinions. But I love when you are listening to each other and learning from each other.

Lucy is pointing out that Jacob said that this looked like a grandma to him, and the little boy, they are together.

19. *Student 1*: I think it's the nanny.
20. *Ms. C*: Okay, so there are some questions, is this the nanny or grandma. . . . They are holding hands and you think they are going on the bus.
21. *Carly*: I agree with him.
22. *Ms. C*: What were you thinking?
23. *Carly*: I was thinking that that was the grandma, and that was the little boy, and they were going on to the bus and that was the last stop.
24. *Ms. C:* Very good, boys and girls. You are making some great predictions!

This exchange shows Ms. Cabana working with students as they make predictions about the book based on the dust jacket. After giving students time to brainstorm and share their thoughts with peers, Ms. Cabana brings the class back together and asks for students to share their predictions about the text. One pair of students, Mateus and Jonas, draws attention to the stickers on the dust jacket, which Ms. Cabana explains is an indication of the award the book received. Sonia, who is identified as an ELL student, discusses the mode of transportation seen on the front of the dust jacket—a bus—and speculates about where the passengers might be going. This suggestion leads to contributions from other students regarding the identity of the passengers, some referring to the older woman as a nanny, and others identifying her as a grandma.

The next exchange is from a class session in which Ms. Cabana guided students through an exploration of the dust jacket of *Dolphins at Daybreak*, a chapter book they worked with for several weeks. Because the book is part of a series, many students were familiar with the main characters, which is why some students reference the characters by name (Jack and Annie) in the following exchange.

1. *Ms. C*: Let's take a look at the cover of this book.
2. *Ben*: By the title, I know there's going to be dolphins because it says dolphins.
3. *Ms. C*: Oh good! That was the first thing I was going to tell you to do was to read the title for me and the title of this book is . . .

4. *Students*: *Dolphins at Daybreak*.

5. *Ms. C*: We can take a hint about where the setting of the story is. The setting of the story would be . . .

6. *Student 1*: The ocean.

7. *Student 2*: The beach.

8. *Ben*: The forest.

9. *Ms. C*: We made a prediction that the story would take place in the ocean. Some of my friends, like Ben, said that actually it'll probably start in the forest because when he opened the book he saw a picture that had lots of trees.

10. *Ms. C*: In chapter books, that happens a lot of times because the setting, where the story takes place, can change. What other predictions do you have about the story? What do you think the story is going to be about? What problem might they have, Sarah?

11. *Sarah*: [no response]

12. *Ms. C*: Remember, when you make a prediction, you are just taking a guess. You look at the picture and the title and you think, "Hmm . . . I wonder . . . ." So, what problem do you think Jack and Annie might have in the story?

13. *Sarah*: [no response]

14. *Ms. C*: Do you think there is anything strange here? What do you think is strange in this picture? Is there anything you think is weird here?

15. *Sarah*: [shakes head no]

16. *Ms. C*: So, have you seen kids in the middle of the ocean with their backpacks on? [references picture on the front dust jacket]

17. *Sarah*: [shakes head no]

18. *Student 3*: No, not with clothes!

19. *Ms. C*: Well, they have their clothes on, and they have their backpacks on, and they are in the middle of the ocean. Do you think this might be a problem?

20. *Lucy*: Yea, because they don't have parents watching them, and they could sink.

21. *Ms. C*: Okay, there are no parents watching.

22. *Student 4*: They might get lost on the beach and the dolphins will help them back.

23. *Student 3*: When I see the picture, they are only holding the top of the fin, so they might fall off the dolphin.
24. *Ms. C*: Okay, any other predictions?
25. *Max*: I think they were stuck in the Pacific Ocean and dolphins came to save them.
26. *Ms. C*: These predictions are great, and they make me have a lot of questions like, "How did they end up in the Pacific Ocean?" "Why are their clothes still on?" Does anyone have questions popping in their mind right now?
27. *Student 5*: Why were they in the ocean?
28. *Ms. C*: Who else has questions?
29. *Lucy*: My question is, "Why are they in the middle of the ocean with no parents and no one watching them?"
30. *Ms. C*: Okay, good. Ben, what question do you have?
31. *Ben*: Are the dolphins bad or good?
32. *Ms. C*: Okay, those are some great questions. Now my question for you all is about the title of our book. What does daybreak mean?
33. *Student 6*: That means that it's going to turn night time.
34. *Student 7*: It's going to be a break in the day.
35. *Ms. C*: Like a break for playground time?
36. *Student 6*: No, daybreak means when it's the time when we don't have to come to school, like spring break.
37. *Student 8:* I think it's when the sun is almost setting.
38. *Ms. C*: So, daybreak is when the sun is setting, and it's about to go down?
39. *Student 9*: Yes, it's like the evening.
40. *Ms. C*: Okay, well, we are going to have to read to find the answers to all of these questions. Are these dolphins good? Why are these kids in the middle of the ocean? What time of day is daybreak?

The two exchanges showcase the ways that Ms. Cabana was able to create opportunities for meaning making in relation to the dust jacket as a promotional peritextual element. The excerpts also demonstrate the multiple ways in which students responded during these initial discussions. In both conversation pieces, students discussed how this element affected their views of the work, responding with descriptions, interpretations and evaluations, predictions, and attention to written language. Students frequently described what they thought was happening in the illustration on the dust jacket of the book and then interpreted that information in order to make predictions regarding the setting, characters, and plot of the stories (e.g., see dialogue 2, lines 19–23). Apart from evaluating the illustrations on the dust jackets of the books, in each of the discussions, students paid close attention to written language in order to facilitate their story predictions. This attention to written language is especially evident in the first exchange of dialogue when students gave their thoughts about the plot of the story (e.g., see dialogue 1, lines 10 and 23).

Although Ms. Cabana was able to facilitate rich and meaningful conversations surrounding these two books, there are additional ways that she could have extended each of the discussions surrounding this peritextual element in order to scaffold students' meaning-making interactions with the dust jackets. For example, in connection to *Last Stop on Market Street*, Ms. Cabana could have identified and shared other books that received the same prestigious award. She also could have incorporated information about the author, potentially sparking students' interest even more. The second book, *Dolphins at Daybreak*, is part of an extensive series, and Ms. Cabana could have spent additional time reviewing stories that students had read previously, probing their knowledge about the different adventures of the two main characters. Ms. Cabana also might have allowed for additional conversation about students' personal experiences in relation to the ocean and dolphins, possibly drawing out their scientific knowledge about ocean animals.

## Further Applications

Based on the rich experiences that Ms. Cabana created for her students, along with areas that we identified that could have been further explored, the following five strategies can be used by elementary educators to purposefully use the dust jackets of illustrated children's literature as a teaching tool.

*Strategy 1:* Prepare for discussions about book dust jackets. As teachers prepare to incorporate illustrated children's books into their lessons, they must also devote time to preparing a discussion about the books' dust jackets. Teachers can do this by carefully examining the peritextual elements of the book dust jacket to uncover the different meaning-making affordances.[24] Once teachers personally discover what book dust jackets have to offer, they will be able to help enrich their students' learning experiences. This process of preparing for discussions about book dust jackets may initially require additional time; however, as these types of discussions become a routine practice, teachers will become more aware of the potential that book dust jackets have to offer, and discussions of this nature will flow more naturally.

*Strategy 2*: Develop a common vocabulary to talk about book dust jackets. Several terms related to illustrated picture book dust jackets are likely to come up in multiple discussions. In order to facilitate the book dust jacket discussions between elementary teachers and students, it is necessary to help students develop a vocabulary to talk about books. Clearly defining terms such as title, author, illustrator, and image and explaining the common awards given to children's literature will ensure a common foundation for these discussions. Gross and Latham provide an extensive list of peritext terms that can be used to facilitate discussions about books.[25] After introducing these terms to students, the teacher will need to make a conscious effort to model the correct use of terminology and actively encourage students to include these terms in their own vocabulary.

*Strategy 3*: Activate prior knowledge using book dust jackets. A third pedagogical strategy that teachers can implement is to use book dust jackets to activate students' prior knowledge by encouraging them to draw on their diverse funds of knowledge,[26] from both their academic and social experiences. When drawing on their academic experiences, students often make intertextual connections to other books and content to which they have been exposed.[27] For example, students may have read a book from the same series or on the same topic. If the book they are discussing has been awarded a medal (e.g., Pura Belpré, Caldecott), students may make a connection to other books to which they have been exposed that also have received this same award. Students may also make intratextual connections as they notice similarities and differences between the verbal and visual elements of the book dust jackets.[28] In addition, students can make personal connections to the book, which promotes their engagement in the discussion and helps build their anticipation of reading the upcoming text.

*Strategy 4*: Make and confirm predictions with book dust jackets. Illustrated book dust jackets offer a great opportunity for teachers to challenge students to go beyond discussing just what they see. Teachers can facilitate discussions related to what students think might be taking place on the book dust jackets, as well as predictions about the story's plot, setting, and characters. These predictions can be encouraged through invitations, encouragements, probes, and predicting questions.[29] Book covers as a peritextual element can offer readers support through activation of prior knowledge, identification of settings and characters, and predictions of what the narrative might be about.[30] In addition, students can continue to use book dust jackets as a meaning-making resource as they read, using the narrative to confirm or disconfirm their predictions. These types of discussions enable children to further develop their critical and creative thinking.[31]

*Strategy 5:* Inspire creativity with book dust jackets. Building on meaningful discussions, teachers can incorporate activities and assignments that allow students to express their creativity vis-à-vis book dust jackets. Students can often benefit from carrying out these activities and assignments in collaboration with their peers. For example, after reading the text and discussing the purpose of book dust jackets and all they can offer, students could come up with an alternative book dust jacket that represents the content of the book, generating a different title, cover picture, and book endorsement.

## Conclusion

This chapter showed examples of how a first-grade teacher led discussions about the dust jackets of a picture book and a beginning chapter book. Students explored how the dust jacket, as a promotional peritextual element, affected their views of the two books. As Ms. Cabana introduced the two books, she facilitated a discussion in which the students were able to comment on the various elements present on the dust jackets and make predictions based on those elements. This study demonstrates how focusing on the dust jackets of books allows teachers to facilitate meaningful interactions with and conversations about literature.

### NOTES

1. Evelyn Arizpe and Morag Styles, *Children Reading Pictures: Interpreting Visual Texts*, 2d ed. (New York: Routledge, 2015).

2. Miriam G. Martinez and Janis M. Harmon, "An Investigation of Teachers' Growing Understandings of the Picture Book Format," *Reading Psychology* 36, no. 4 (2015): 299–314, doi:10.1080/02702711.2013.843066.

3. Martinez and Harmon, "An Investigation."

4. Grace Enriquez, Summer R. Clark, and Jessica Della Calce, "Using Children's Literature for Dynamic Learning Frames and Growth Mindsets," *Reading Teacher* 70, no. 6 (2017): 711–19, doi:10.1002/trtr.1583; Lawrence R. Sipe, *Storytime: Young Children's Literary Understanding in the Classroom* (New York: Teachers College Press, 2008).

5. Pauline Gibbons, *Scaffolding Language, Scaffolding Learning: Teaching English Language Learners in the Mainstream Classroom*, 2d ed. (Portsmouth, NH: Heinemann, 2015).

6. Patricia A. Ganea, Lili Ma, and Judy S. DeLoache, "Young Children's Learning and Transfer of Biological Information from Picture Books to Real Animals," *Child Development* 82, no. 5 (2011): 1421–33, doi:10.1111/j.1467-8624.2011 .01612.x; Joyce Shatzer, "Picture Book Power: Connecting Children's Literature and Mathematics," *Reading Teacher* 61, no. 8 (2008): 649–53, doi:10.1598/ RT.61.8.6.

7. Miriam Martinez, Catherine Stier, and Lori Falcon, "Judging a Book by Its Cover: An Investigation of Peritextual Features in Caldecott Award Books," *Children's Literature in Education* 47, no. 3 (2016): 225–41, doi:10.1007/s10583-016-9272-8; Sipe, Storytime.

8. Martinez, Stier, and Falcon, "Judging a Book"; Sipe, *Storytime.*

9. See, for example, Martinez, Stier, and Falcon, "Judging a Book"; Sipe, *Storytime.*

10. Martinez, Stier, and Falcon, "Judging a Book."

11. Gérard Genette, *Paratexts: Thresholds of Interpretation* (New York: Cambridge University Press, 1997).

12. Genette, *Paratexts.*

13. Margaret R. Higonnet, "The Playground of the Peritext," *Children's Literature Association Quarterly* 15, no. 2 (1990): 47–49, doi:10.1353/chq.0.0831; Martinez, Stier, and Falcon, "Judging a Book"; Sipe, *Storytime.*

14. Melissa Gross, Don Latham, Jennifer Underhill, and Hyerin Bak, "The Peritext Book Club: Reading to Foster Critical Thinking about STEAM Texts," *School Library Research* 19 (October 28, 2016): 1–17, www.ala.org/aasl/slr; Sipe, *Storytime.*

15. Higonnet, "The Playground of the Peritext."

16. Sipe, *Storytime.*

17. Genette, *Paratexts.*

18. Melissa Gross and Don Latham, "The Peritextual Literacy Framework: Using the Functions of Peritext to Support Critical Thinking," *Library and Information Science Research* 39, no. 2 (2017): 116–23.

19. Gross, Latham, Underhill, and Bak, "The Peritext Book Club."

20. Shelbie Witte, Melissa Gross, and Don Latham, "Using the Peritextual Literacy Framework with Young Adult Biographies: Introducing Peritextual Functions with Adolescents in Social Studies," in *Adolescent Literature as a Complement to the Content Areas: Social Science and the Humanities,* ed. Paula Greathouse, Joan F. Kaywell, and Joyce Eisenbach, 69–82 (London, UK: Rowman and Littlefield, 2017).

21. Gross and Latham, "The Peritextual Literacy Framework."

22. Matt de la Peña, *Last Stop on Market Street* (London, UK: Penguin Books, 2015).

23. Mary Pope Osborne, *Dolphins at Daybreak* (New York: Random House Children's Books, 1997).

24. Martinez, Stier, and Falcon, "Judging a Book."

25. Gross and Latham, "The Peritextual Literacy Framework."

26. Norma González, Luis C. Moll, and Cathy Amanti, *Funds of Knowledge: Theorizing Practices in Households, Communities, and Classrooms* (New York: Routledge, 2005).

27. Lawrence R. Sipe and Caroline E. McGuire, "Picturebook Endpapers: Resources for Literary and Aesthetic Interpretation," *Children's Literature in Education: An International Quarterly* 37, no. 4 (2006): 291–304; Witte, Gross, and Latham, "Using the Peritextual Literacy Framework."

28. Sipe and McGuire, "Picturebook Endpapers"; Witte, Gross, and Latham, "Using the Peritextual Literacy Framework."

29. Sipe, *Storytime*.

30. Sipe, *Storytime*; Martinez, Stier, and Falcon, "Judging a Book."

31. Sipe, *Storytime*.

$$9$$

# Cathy's Book and the Boundaries of Books in a Participatory Age

## Exploring Pedagogies and Paratexts in Expansive Contexts

ANTERO GARCIA AND BUD HUNT

FROM THE MOMENT YOU OR YOUR STUDENTS OPEN THE BOOK, YOU'VE MADE a transgressive action as a reader. The first part of the book's title—*Cathy's Book*—denotes that this isn't yours. Do you open the book, taking a peek? The second part offers you a bit of guided instruction: *If Found Call (650) 266–8233*. Perhaps you look over the seemingly real number, dubious. Then again, you did find the book . . . maybe give it a ring? A moment later an adolescent voice informs you to leave a message: "Hey, this is Cathy and I can't come to the phone right now. . . ." You listen to the eerie message and wonder (even before turning a page of the book): what and how am I reading?

The young adult novel *Cathy's Book*[1] is a bold challenge to how textual engagement and reading shift in a participatory and connected culture.[2] As a book that intentionally expands where and how a novel is read, the work's central conceit in this regard is found in the novel's subtitle: *If Found Call (650) 266–8233*. Indeed, dialing the number leads readers to a working phone number as do several other numbers found throughout the book. Likewise, marginalia such as notes, doodles, and ongoing conversational reminders add a commentary layered throughout a larger narrative. To "read" *Cathy's Book* is to engage in activities that expand beyond the pages of the book. Its text lives in printed words, in scribbled notes, in photographed images, and—as implied by its subtitle—in phone numbers and digital ephemera that move the book beyond what is found within its pages.

Taking Gérard Genette's definition and using *Cathy's Book* as an example, this chapter highlights how authorship in today's era of connected learning[3] pushes peritexts beyond the physical limitations of a book. Though peritexts historically have been anchored by a book's dimensions, *Cathy's Book* emphasizes the possibilities of books being bigger than their physical boundaries might imply. Ultimately, this chapter uses this novel to highlight implications of paratextual reading, writing, and community building for classroom settings. The authors of this chapter, a university researcher and an instructional technologist who are both former high school language arts teachers, have explored texts like these with students in our high school classrooms.

## Connected Paratexts in a Participatory Age

Genette's description of paratext within print-based works helps guide our initial understanding of how to read and teach a book like *Cathy's Book*:

> Text is rarely presented in an unadorned state, unreinforced and unaccompanied by a certain number of verbal or other productions, such as an author's name, a title, a preface, illustrations . . . they surround it and extend it, precisely in order to present it, in the usual sense of the verb but also in the strongest sense: to make present, to ensure the text's presence in the world, its "reception" and consumption in the form (nowadays, at least) of a book.[4]

The framing of paratexts here acts as the foundation from which we consider how paratexts—both conceptually and practically—have changed over time. From an educational stance, Genette's definition offers powerful opportunities to expand readers' assumptions about what reading looks like and what processes, materials, and textual practices form reading. As Melissa Gross and Don Latham write,

> Examination of paratext allows the reader to think critically about the author['s] or creator's intent as well as the veracity of the work, and, when used to consider a work, can allow readers to reflect on the role of individual paratextual elements that help the reader to identify, navigate, and connect

the work to the reader's interest as well as the resources that support the author's presentation.[5]

As we explore how previous research and this chapter's current emphasis on *Cathy's Book* expand what paratexts mean in the reading experiences of individuals and their pedagogic demands, we also want to recognize that such shifts were also predicted by Genette.

Genette's parenthetical nod to "nowadays" is a prescient one. Looking at this explanation two decades later, the role of paratext still largely holds true to Genette's description. However, what counts as a book, as a text, and as the necessary "verbal and other productions" in digital and nondigital contexts is striking. Since Genette's first description of paratexts, the fields of education and of literacies have expanded substantially. Recognizing the important role of multimodal literacies and multiliteracies in the increasingly digital and wireless contexts of socialization, learning, and commerce,[6] understandably, what is read and published, and how, shift continually over time. Likewise, recent educational research has explored informal learning practices of youth in "connected" contexts,[7] recognizing the possibilities of pedagogy when considering how youth engage in learning practices that are "socially embedded, interest-driven, and oriented toward educational, economic, or political opportunity."[8]

Questions about how reading and texts are constructed must be revisited regularly in light of connected learning and emerging new literacies. What, for instance, is the role of hashtags as mediating, organizing, and clarifying text in how new reading platforms redefine traditional textual and paratextual features?[9] Similarly, in considering how transmedia reshapes reading, Amy Nottingham-Martin questions where paratextual elements are derived from and whether a "particular element [builds] the narrative from within, or does it comment on the narrative from an outside perspective of awareness of the narrative itself as an entity?"[10]

Various efforts have been made to catalog kinds of para- and peritextual elements across different media, genres, and contexts.[11] Constructing a "Peritextual Literacy Framework," Gross and Latham list six different types of peritexts that allow "for the analysis of peritextual elements by how they are positioned in relation to the text and for peritextual elements to be understood and discussed based on their function or purpose in relation to the work."[12]

## DEFINING *CATHY'S BOOK: IF FOUND CALL (650) 266–8233*

*Cathy's Book* is presented as a found diary of 16-year-old Cathy that relates her experiences with a mysterious, and slightly older, man named Victor who, after a couple of dates, vanishes and begins to avoid Cathy's calls and texts. Cathy collects several artifacts (which we will explore further later in this chapter) as she investigates what happened to Victor, and her discoveries lead her into a bigger mystery.

However, although the story itself falls into familiar romantic, dramatic, and action tropes found in many young adult (YA) novels, its form is something of a harbinger of how reading practices and youth interactions with paratexts are changing. In particular, we want to consider where the text of *Cathy's Book* is found. On the one hand, the 143 pages of the text contain a fundamental novel. Read on its own, there is a sound beginning, middle, and end to the text. However, *Cathy's Book* does not follow the paratextual conventions of most novels that came before it, suggesting that the "nowadays" of Genette's 1997 work may be brushing against new modalities and practices of book authorship, production, and consumption.

In order to determine the paratextual practices within *Cathy's Book*, we want to first identify four different components that comprise reading the novel:

1. *Cathy's Book:* The bulk of the printed novel is presented as a non-linear diary written by teenager and developing artist Cathy Vickers. However, in addition to her day-to-day (sometimes hour-to-hour) recounting of her life, this diary includes her annotations—underlined passages, asides, and reminders. Further, for a key section of the book, Cathy presents lengthy text messages exchanged with two other characters, making her diary one that reconstructs multimodal messages with other characters. The book also includes doodles in the marginalia and drawings of key incidents that are described. These layers—Cathy's narrative, her notes, and her drawings—comprise the main elements of the printed text.

2. *Images, endpapers, and other physical artifacts: Cathy's Book* was first published with a set of tangible artifacts: maps, photographs, a death certificate, a takeout menu, and other ephemera that directly and indirectly tied into the narrative that Cathy offers. These artifacts are printed as high-resolution pages in the center of the book and

behind the book's cover in the most recent edition. These items are not offered with captions or labeled with any specific reference to passages in the book. A reader might believe the items to be supplemental, though, as we will argue, that simply is not the case.

3. *Audio content:* The phone number in the book's title is one of nearly a dozen numbers that can be called. A bit of sleuthing and searching through the book yields the passcodes to Cathy's and other characters' voice mail, allowing readers to discover messages left for the characters.

4. *Online material:* Finally, many of the companies and locations described in the book have websites that were created as part of this book (e.g., www.intrepidbiotech.com/—a common practice in other alternate reality narratives and games.[13] In addition, several of the locations and items described in the book actually exist, inviting readers to discover San Francisco Bay–area locations such as the Musée Mécanique. Finally, there are official web pages (and a still-active discussion forum) for readers to discuss and share hints about how to best read *Cathy's Book*. As with the physical artifacts, these elements may appear to be aligned with Genette's framing of epitext; however, they too, remain central to the narrative at the heart of *Cathy's Book*.

## TEACHING *CATHY'S BOOK*

In looking across what makes up *Cathy's Book*, we recognize that our descriptions of searching, seeking hints, and unlocking aspects of the story portray *Cathy's Book* as gamelike. Further, the authors are also responsible for constructing notable alternate reality games prior to publishing this novel.[14] However, we want to emphasize that this is a novel. It has gamelike elements that point to new genres of storytelling and immersion more than a blurring between book and gaming media. Though readers could read the entire print-based book without the scraps or inserts or audio content, they would miss substantial elucidation on moments within and beyond the printed story. Bud Hunt, one of the authors of this chapter, learned this aspect particularly after the experience of teaching this text in a tenth-grade literature course. When Hunt first discovered the novel as a high school language arts teacher, and ultimately taught it as a novel in his tenth-grade literature course, the text raised questions about what it means to teach a text as well as what counted as text. The book entered his classroom a bit by accident. We reflect on the in-the-moment experiences teaching *Cathy's Book* in an alternative high school more than a decade ago:

> There are only two students in the class at the moment, and we've been together for nine weeks, so we're starting to get used to each other as readers and thinkers.
>
> We pick the books that we're reading together, and so it was a pretty normal day when we arrived at a local book store to pick out our next text, as well as some new books for the library that I had ordered.
>
> Of course, the book we had selected wasn't in. But we found something else.
>
> A student handed me a black, hard cover book, with the words *Cathy's Book: If found call (650) 266–8233* written with what appeared to be silver marker on the cover. She asked me what I thought. On a hunch, I asked her if she had her cell phone with her. She pulled it from her pocket, at which point I instructed her to dial the number.
>
> She was nervous about that, so she asked me to instead. . . .
>
> From the moment we heard that message, we were curious. Then, we opened the book. Alongside a pretty standard looking book was a pouch full of documents and other stuff: ripped up photographs, a menu, some old letters, and some other odd items. We shared the find with the other student in the class, dialed the number for her, she took a listen, and we headed to the register with our new read in hand.[15]

Later in the same post, Hunt articulated what confirmed his sense that this text isn't complete without the stuff beyond the codex:

> *Cathy's Book* is a puzzle wrapped inside a book and scattered around lots of voice mail boxes, collections of documents, websites, and . . . well, we're not sure what else yet. We just know it's addictive and contagious. At least one other student here at school is waiting to read the book, and we're all reading voraciously; we even met up today during lunch to check in on the progress that we've each made. (All of us had discovered different clues that allowed us to access various hidden puzzles. We needed each other to make the picture begin to be complete. VERY COOL.)[16]

As an "addictive and contagious" reading experience, *Cathy's Book* is a narrative that is—through exploration—discovered. Each additional element that is found, unlocked, or deciphered becomes a part of the text itself. When the paratext is a fundamental part of the story, composed by a character from the story, is the paratext still para, or is it just text? Instruction that allows students to investigate these questions based on their own interpretations can shift how young people read and exude expertise in classrooms today.

## READING, PLAYING, AND SUPPLEMENTING

Expanding on A. Rockenberger's description of peri- and paratext within video games, we believe that new media genres ultimately challenge the way that teachers and students approach the relationship between a text and the materials that "surround it and extend it."[17] The paratext of *Cathy's Book*—the doodles, phone numbers, takeout menus, and the like—are not supplemental to a written narrative. They are the narrative and equally as substantive.

Describing the Peritextual Literacy Framework, Gross and Latham highlight how peritextual elements typically "expand understanding" of a text and "can be analyzed to discern how they work to extend and deepen the body of the work as well as how they help the work achieve its goals."[18] Most books that students have historically encountered in schools conform to these pedagogical opportunities. *Cathy's Book* still provides standard peritextual elements (e.g., titles, blurbs, and endorsements) for students to explore. However, more important, this novel heralds new ways that texts creep into the stuff that surrounds them. Texts must be taught as existing across expansive media in light of the participatory elements of the novel.

Further, the assumption that physical objects and online materials are supplemental—rather than foundational—to a novel like *Cathy's Book* may not represent the direction of youth-oriented texts in the future. The proposition of extra materials adding to context assumes an archaic frame of what in a book is most important; when a website or a collection of purportedly found objects anchors a narrative just as much as a printed and bound book, past assumptions of what form a text takes must be rethought. English language arts contexts in particular tend to value words—specifically, words that are ordered in Western conventions and (ideally) drafted in standard English. In contrast, considering *Cathy's Book* demonstrates that reading does not need to center words or their presentation in traditional book-based formats. In all its spatial constellations, this book illustrates that meaning is found in the assemblage of threads that must be woven across space, time, and modalities.

## Conclusion: Beyond the Mind's Eye

One strategy that English language arts teachers often teach to their students is to picture the characters and actions in a story in one's mind's eye. However, in considering the role of paratextual construction across the story of Cathy Vickers, this strategy must be reconsidered in the contemporary age. By looking at the images that Cathy doodles and the photographs presented, and listening to the audio messages that are a part of this book, readers can know what the characters look like and sound like. The book highlights how some forms of imagination could become dead ends for readers today while others—skipping, reading, playing intellectual hopscotch across media—become possible. Further, these possibilities are temporally bound.

Reading *Cathy's Book* a dozen years after its initial release, it is interesting to consider the ways the book—in all of its elements—has aged. Many of the websites about the book and as part of the book rely on Flash and do not necessarily run as seamlessly as they did at the book's initial release. Likewise, considering how foundational text messaging, private messaging apps, and other forms of communication may be in the lives of teenagers today,[19] actually calling a phone number—let alone leaving a voice mail—seems almost archaic.

The playfulness of writing and telling stories is one to encourage in terms of instruction across new media. How do students in classrooms replicate the expansive opportunities of *Cathy's Book* in their own writing? The Skeleton Creek novels include short films that are interspersed within each book, weaving together stories across media. Likewise, the adult horror novel *House of Leaves* plays with text and layout but also emphasizes footnotes as a foundational aspect of where the book's narrative is more likely to be found. How do similar books like the Skeleton Creek series, *House of Leaves*, or *Ship of Theseus* (a book packaged as a novel with two sets of annotations in dialogue with one another) highlight how books continually challenge materiality, past conventions, and future pathways for the book? *Cathy's Book* acts as harbinger of new possibilities not only for reading and redefining paratextual conventions but also for how youth write and interact today.

## NOTES

1. Sean Stewart and Jordan Weisman, *Cathy's Book: If Found Call (650) 266–8233* (Philadelphia: Running Press, 2006).

2. Henry Jenkins, *Convergence Culture: Where Old and New Media Collide* (New York: New York University Press, 2006); Henry Jenkins, Katie Clinton, Ravi Purushotma, Alice J. Robison, and Margaret Weigel, *Confronting the Challenges of Participatory Culture: Media Education for the 21st Century* (Chicago: MacArthur Foundation, 2009).

3. Antero Garcia, ed., *Teaching in the Connected Learning Classroom* (Irvine, CA: Digital Media and Learning Research Hub, 2014); Mimi Ito, Kris Gutiérrez, Sonia Livingstone, Bill Penuel, J. Rhodes, Katie Salen, . . . and S. Craig Watkins, *Connected Learning: An Agenda for Research and Design* (Irvine, CA: Digital Media and Learning Research Hub, 2013).

4. Gérard Genette, *Paratexts: Thresholds of Interpretation* (New York: Cambridge University Press, 1997), 1.

5. Melissa Gross and Don Latham, "The Peritextual Literacy Framework: Using the Functions of Peritext to Support Critical Thinking," *Library and Information Science Research* 39, no. 2 (2017): 116.

6. See, for example, Colin Lankshear and Michelle Knobel, *New Literacies: Everyday Practices and Social Learning* (New York: Open University Press, 2011); New London Group, "A Pedagogy of Multiliteracies: Designing Social Futures," *Harvard Education Review* 66, no. 1 (1996): 60–92.

7. See, for example, Garcia, *Teaching in the Connected Learning Classroom*; Ito et al., *Connected Learning*.

8. Ito et al., *Connected Learning*, 6.

9. Antero Garcia, "Networked Teens and YA Literature: Gossip, Identity, and What Really #Matters," *ALAN Review* (2016); R. Santo, "Hacker Literacies: User-Generated Resistance and Reconfiguration of Networked Publics," in *Critical Digital Literacies as Social Praxis: Intersections and Challenges,* ed. J. Ávila and J. Z. Pandya (New York: Peter Lang, 2012).

10. Amy Nottingham-Martin, "Thresholds of Transmedia Storytelling," in *Gamification: Concepts, Methodologies, Tools, and Applications*, ed. Information Resources Management Association (2015): 832, quoted in Gross and Latham, "The Peritextual Literacy Framework," 292.

11. See, for example, Gross and Latham, "The Peritextual Literacy Framework"; A. Rockenberger, "Video Game Framings," in *Examining Paratextual Theory and Its Applications in Digital Culture*, ed. N. Desrochers and D. Apollon (Hershey, PA: IGI Global, 2014), 252–86.

12. Gross and Latham, "The Peritextual Literacy Framework," 116.

13. Antero Garcia and Greg Niemeyer, eds., *Virtual, Visible, and Viable: Alternate Reality Games and the Cusp of Digital Gameplay* (New York: Bloomsbury, 2017).

14. Sean Stewart, "Collaborating with the Audience: Alternate Reality Games," Sean Stewart (blog), 2006, www.seanstewart.org/collaborating-with-the-audience-alternate-reality-games.

15. B. Hunt, "Have You Seen Cathy's Book?," *Bud the Teacher* (blog), October 27, 2006, http://budtheteacher.com/blog/2006/10/27/have-you-seen-cathys-book.

16. Hunt, "Have You Seen Cathy's Book?"

17. Genette, *Paratexts*, 1.

18. Gross and Latham, "The Peritextual Literacy Framework," 119.

19. Garcia, "Networked Teens and YA Literature."

# PART IV

# PERITEXTUAL ANALYSIS OF NONPRINT TEXTS

# Analyzing Online News Articles Using Peritextual Elements

## HYERIN BAK AND JOSEY MCDANIEL

FOLLOWING THE 2016 ELECTION, NEW TERMS SUCH AS *FAKE NEWS* AND *alternative facts* have been commonly used to refer to news articles "that are intentionally and verifiably false, and could mislead readers."[1] A false story is shared quickly through social media. The majority of American adults consume news from a single source, particularly on social media such as Facebook.[2] It can be taken for granted that many people read news in a digital form these days.[3]

Many sources have claimed that the news plays an important role in preserving democracy and in informing self-governing citizens.[4] In this era of trust issues, more attention is being paid to the concept of news literacy in media literacy education. News literacy is considered a specialized category of media literacy.[5] It is defined as an "ability to use critical thinking skills to judge the reliability and credibility of news reports, whether they come via print, TV, or the Internet."[6] In 2003, the National Council of Teachers of English (NCTE) passed a resolution encouraging "preservice, inservice, and staff development programs that will focus on new literacies, multimedia composition, and a broadened concept of literacy."[7] The increasing importance of news literacy education has led to media-literacy education initiatives in an attempt to implement news literacy instruction for students.

The BBC School Report program gave students ages 11 to 18 across the UK the chance to engage in the practice of news production.[8] However, the students did not learn news analysis, so they did not demonstrate knowledge of news-related concepts, such as credibility, bias, and fairness.[9] The BBC is launching a new project to teach young people how to identify fake news or false information.[10]

Other initiatives provide programs that bring experienced journalists to classrooms and the public. [11] Students in grades K–12 and college learn how to judge the reliability and credibility of news sources. These programs focus on teaching skills to distinguish fact from fiction. With this background, the Peritextual Literacy Framework (PLF) can be easily adopted by teachers or librarians in the public education sector for teaching K–12 students how to evaluate news.

## Statement of Problem

The skills for news literacy are relevant to information literacy, media literacy, and critical thinking skills. Evaluating information critically and competently is the key skill that the concepts of information literacy and critical thinking have emphasized as well.[12] Media-literacy skills also include analyzing messages in media.[13] Renee Hobbs viewed critical-reading and critical-viewing skills as part of media-literacy education for modern citizens.[14] They should be able to develop their critical-thinking skills and to identify high-quality news sources by having opportunities to learn related skills during media-literacy education.[15] For any level of news-literacy education, it is recommended that teachers "connect comprehension and analysis"[16] and "ask critical questions and listen well"[17] rather than focusing on teaching appreciation for news and journalism.

The Peritextual Literacy Framework (PLF) can be employed for news literacy education in classrooms. The PLF is "a tool for accessing, evaluating, and comprehending the content of media using elements that frame the body of a work and mediate its content for the user."[18] The PLF has not been applied to news media, but it may support critical thinking–related skills focusing on information evaluation.[19] Students can use the PLF in the online news environment to critically evaluate and analyze the information and to determine credible sources for their learning or their daily life. The PLF can provide K–12 classes with a practical guideline for analyzing news articles.

This study aims to modify the PLF for online news articles and to demonstrate the application of peritextual elements to online news reading in order to foster critical thinking. Based on student feedback, instructional methods or assessment methods can be refined.

## Evaluating News

It was found that university students who were exposed to a short media literacy presentation that taught the news process and interpretation of a news story were less likely to perceive a news story about a controversial issue as biased.[20] For evaluation of news, teachers at Stony Brook University taught the Deconstruction Guide, which directed students to analyze news through eight steps, such as "Assess the evidence supporting the main points of the story. Was it verified?" and "Does the reporter place the story in context?"[21] Even though the study was contextualized at a college level, it has implications for secondary students as well because the program taught students how to access news, evaluate and analyze news, and appreciate a specific genre of news.

Because online news is a part of online information that requires reasoning skills, the report by the Stanford History Education Group is relevant.[22] The study revealed that less than 20 percent of high school students were able to recognize that a given post on a photo-sharing website did not provide strong evidence and to locate key details such as the source of the photo. In general, the report showed that students had trouble judging the credibility or reliability of information online by recognizing sponsored content or political biases.

## Peritextual Elements in Online News Articles

The PLF is based on Gérard Genette's paratext theory.[23] Genette defined paratext as consisting of peritextual elements that appear within the text and epitextual elements that exist outside the text.[24]

The PLF has not yet been used for an analysis of online news articles. Dorothee Birke and Birte Christ analyzed e-books using the items' paratext.[25] The researchers stated that digital narratives have elements with functions that print materials did not provide in the past. For example, the researchers considered hyperlinks as new elements and functions. People believe that hyperlinks in news articles can generate trust, regardless of whether people click on them.[26]

News articles have their own peritextual elements, such as a headline, a byline with a news provider or press agency, and a lead. Online news articles also differ from printed news articles because of the online articles' unique production methods.[27] For example, "tagging stories and tailoring headlines"[28] have become critical for news reports to be easily found on a search engine or on the web. In addition, online news articles can combine a variety of multimedia elements, such as "hypertext to link to information, video, audio, still images, audio slideshows, animation, interactivity, community elements such as polls, forums, social networks, blogs, data, maps, timelines, FAQs and Q&As, [and] user-generated content."[29]

Melissa Gross and Don Latham categorized six types of peritext according to function and provided examples of peritextual elements that can be found in printed books.[30] The six types are production, promotional, navigational, intratextual, supplemental, and documentary peritext.[31] Considering peritextual elements that can be found in online news articles, this study determined that four types of peritext (production, promotional, supplemental, documentary) can be useful in news literacy education because they can explain a majority of elements in online news articles. By modifying the PLF table developed by Gross and Latham,[32] we developed the Peritextual Elements in Online News Articles table (appendix A).

## Four Peritextual Types in Online News Articles

Production peritext uniquely identifies a work.[33] Production elements in online news articles include headlines, bylines, and the news agency or press agency or news aggregator. Considerations include whether the headline includes the whole story and provides the context and whether it is sponsored content.

Promotional peritext includes elements that interface between the work and its potential audience.[34] Examples are a reporter's biography, hyperlinks to the author's website or social media accounts, and a blurb/bla-bla that advertises the article itself.

Supplemental elements are outside the text proper and augment understanding of the content.[35] They include still images, audio, video, maps, tables, time lines, charts, and comments. Considerations include how the elements help readers understand the work better and whether those elements match the text's content.

Documentary elements connect the audience to external works used to produce the work or those that reify or extend the work's content.[36] In online news articles, documentary elements include hyperlinks, image credits, captions, source notes, and related articles. Readers need to consider whether the article is based on credible sources, whether the sources help them verify the story, and whether it is clear where the information came from. Readers need to consider how the existence of all these types of peritext affects their views of the article.

## Context

The authors of this chapter are a doctoral student in information studies (Bak) and a high school English language arts teacher (McDaniel). Bak proposed the idea of applying peritextual analysis to reading online news articles, and McDaniel found that it would be an interesting lesson for her English classes. Bak designed class materials and discussed them with McDaniel, who knows her students' interests and abilities. During implementation, McDaniel instructed the students and Bak visited the school to observe the classroom instruction and collect students' learning artifacts.

The school is a public high school located in a suburban area in Florida. It houses an average of about two thousand students and one hundred instructors. The main purpose of the school is to prepare students for college, with a heavy focus on Advanced Placement (AP) and college-level offerings. McDaniel teaches 175 students in six sections: four sections of English III and two sections of English IV designated as College Readiness. There is no honors-level English course for senior students; they have the option of taking either AP classes to earn college credit or English IV College Readiness to be gradually introduced to the complexity of work expected of them at the college level. The average class size is twenty-eight students. All 175 students completed the project that applies the PLF to reading online news articles, but only twenty-seven students are in the study.

The students learn about reading news articles through the nonfiction component of English, often studying various articles in the context of connecting literature to world issues. Some students who require remedial reading in order to pass the Florida Standards Assessment examination in the spring have an additional reading class that focuses solely on nonfiction articles.

The students use Edmodo (figure 10.1) as a learning tool for various classes. Edmodo enables teachers to post online assignments and link those assignments to outside sources for easy accessibility and grading. For the peritext project, students were able to locate a Microsoft Word document with the assignment instructions and hyperlinks to access the article for analysis. This was the first time the students were exposed to peritext; many students have been taught for years to focus on reading articles for comprehension and to completely ignore additional elements because they were considered superfluous.

FIGURE 10.1 **Edmodo screenshot**

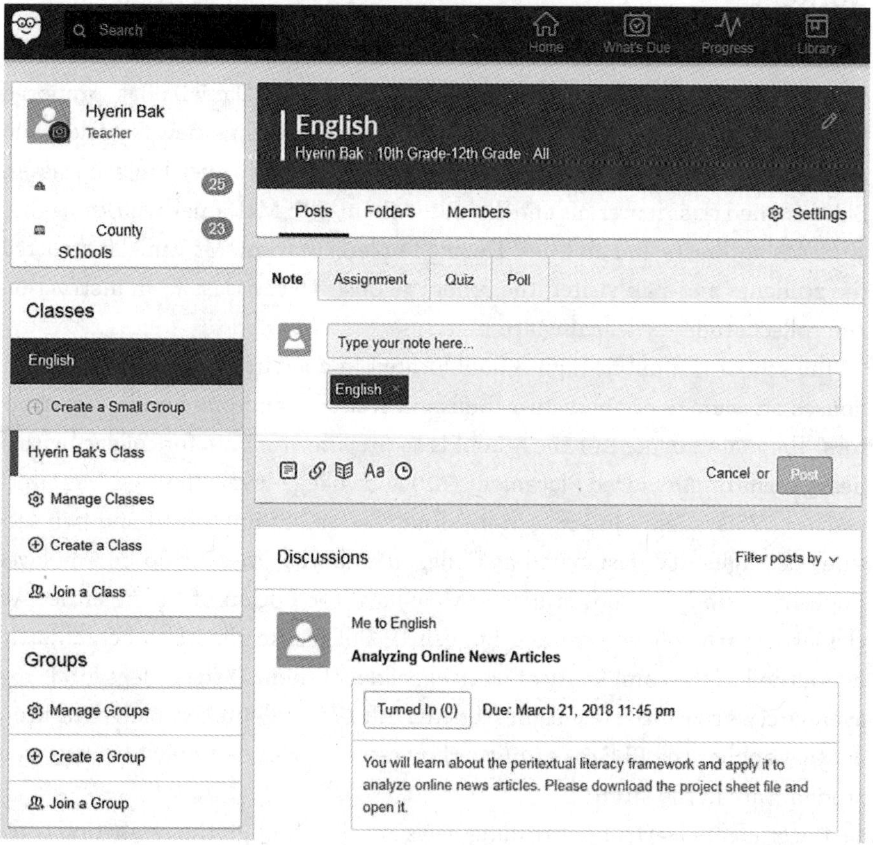

## Application of Idea

The lessons were implemented over three consecutive classes to provide students with enough time to become familiar with the framework and its application. Students used project sheets (see appendix B) for two class periods to provide data for later analysis.

We selected two different online news articles for class activities. These articles differ in terms of topics, news providers, web interfaces, and their peritextual elements. It was expected that students could experience and be prepared to apply the framework in different contexts in their future news reading by analyzing articles with varied peritextual elements.

The news articles for class activities were taken from accountable news sources that have explicit editorial policies and ethical standards. Sources included the BBC, *The Guardian*, the *New York Times*, National Public Radio (NPR), the *Los Angeles Times*, and the *Wall Street Journal*. The news articles were chosen considering timeliness and interest to support student engagement in reading and analyzing the reports.

The first article is online on the *New York Times* website and deals with a recent issue in weather. [37] The second article is online on the BBC News website.[38] Compared to the first article, the second article deals with a relatively political issue and includes more varied supplemental and documentary peritextual elements, such as videos, tweets, and hyperlinks to external sources.

Project sheets were developed that presented a modified version of the Peritextual Literacy Framework (see appendix A) and questions that guided student reading of online news articles (see appendix B). Students were encouraged to access a news article through a hyperlink and scan peritextual elements within the article while skimming it.

Students were then asked to use the guiding questions to analyze the usefulness of the production, promotional, supplemental, and documentary peritextual elements, respectively. Each peritext type had the same set of questions. For example, for the production peritext, the following questions were asked:

- What are the production peritextual elements in the article?
- What do the production peritextual elements tell you?
- Is production peritext helpful to better understand the news article? Why or why not?

This exercise can be helpful for students to evaluate a news article in relation to relevance, credibility, and usability. Thus, the final question in the project sheet was the following:

- Do you think peritextual elements in online news articles help you to better understand your online news reading? Why or why not?

This question can provide students with an opportunity to analyze the news article as a whole and to reflect on their learning so that they can apply the framework to their online news reading in the future.

## DAY 1

On the first day, McDaniel introduced the PLF focusing on the definition of peritext as elements that surround the main body of a published work. She mentioned title, author names, images, and citation information as examples of peritextual elements, regardless of media type, in order that students could understand the concept of peritext. The students were asked to write down the definition of peritext in their notes.

McDaniel then explained that four types of peritext can be found commonly in online news articles, and she briefly introduced each type of peritext. While displaying the Peritextual Elements in Online News Articles table (see appendix A) on the large screen for the class, McDaniel explained the definition of each peritext type and read example elements. Finally, she reviewed what could be considered for each peritext type. This instruction did not require the whole class period. The teacher wanted to expose the students to peritext in order to prepare them for their next class activity in which they would be asked to consider the role of different peritextual elements that are part of online news articles using the framework as a scaffold. The students appeared to understand the concept of peritext at the end of this class session.

## DAY 2 AND DAY 3

In the subsequent class meetings, students convened in a computer lab where each student could access online news articles for the class activities. The students were provided with a print copy of the Peritextual Elements in Online News Articles table (see appendix A). On the board in Edmodo, they could access the project sheet, including the guiding questions. During the fifty minutes of class time, the students were assigned one news article to analyze.

Instead of reading the news articles in depth, the students were encouraged to focus on identifying the various peritextual elements in the news articles and analyze what the elements indicated. They wrote answers for the questions in their notes and turned them in individually.

Students repeated the process with a different news article the next day. On the second day, McDaniel reminded the students of the definition of peritext. While individually reading the framework table and the inquiries on the project sheet, students were encouraged to ask the teacher questions. According to observations, a few students were confused and asked questions such as, "What is a news provider in this article?" and "What is the production peritext here?" Another student needed clarification to distinguish between a peritext type and a peritextual element. When the teacher located the element on the screen and pointed to a relevant peritext type in the framework table, the student understood it easily. Once students were introduced to and had a solid understanding of the peritext as it contributed to the comprehension of the overall article, the assignment seemed to be easier to digest.

On the third day (Day 3), students were given the option to complete the project sheet in pairs. Many students preferred to work individually, but several students worked with a partner in order to discuss what they had found from the news articles. We observed that these students briefly discussed the news websites or a topic dealt with in the news articles as well as the project sheet questions. A few students expressed that it was a little boring to do the same activity for two days.

The time the students took to complete the project sheet and the length of answers varied. It seemed to depend on the individual student and which news article that student was working on. It took less than thirty minutes for some students to complete the task while other students wanted more time to finish their answers. The students had to spend some time locating certain peritextual elements in the article by scrolling down and up the web page and writing down their answers.

According to the worksheet responses, some students were confused by the varying implications of different peritext types. However, most students were positive that the peritextual elements could be a useful tool for their online news reading because these elements help readers pay attention to both "the main idea" and the "more important details" of news articles.

## PRE- AND POST-INTERVENTION SURVEYS

For a summative assessment, pre- and post-intervention surveys in a paper-quiz format were administered to evaluate students' learning of the concepts. The students were asked to define and describe the concepts of the Peritextual Literacy Framework and each type of peritext and to provide example elements of each peritext type.

Pre-intervention survey results indicated that only one of fourteen students was able to guess the definition of the PLF. Results of the post-intervention survey, administered at the end of the third class, showed that eight of fourteen students (57.1 percent) were able to successfully define the PLF. In addition, nine of fourteen students (64.3 percent) were able to define production, promotional, and documentary peritext and to provide at least one example element for each peritext type. Eight students (57.1 percent) did so for the supplemental peritext.

## REFLECTION TO IMPROVE THE LESSON

The instructional strategy presented in this lesson can be improved in several ways. For instance, more time spent in instructional interventions and further development of class materials will help effectively introduce the concept of peritext. Also, time should be spent introducing the concept of viewing articles online and discussing the purpose of peritextual elements. Students will not necessarily immediately understand the word *peritext* without scaffolding to ensure that they recognize that peritext is something they see every day, even if they have not paid close attention to it. It could be interesting and helpful to explore instances of peritext in books, movies, games, and CDs and find out how students use or ignore the information that these elements provide.

In addition, before giving an assignment, the teacher should assess students' knowledge of terms used in online news articles and demonstrate how to answer questions on the project sheet. For example, a teacher can display an example of a news article on the screen, point to "Google News" on the screen, and label it as a news aggregator. The teacher then can revisit the PLF table and have students recognize the element as an example of production peritext because it identifies the work. In order to model the class activities, a teacher can work through a few examples with the class and discuss the usefulness of particular peritextual elements.

Active learning strategies should be considered, when the class environment permits, to motivate students' learning activities. In one such strategy, the peritextual elements table can have blank cells, and students in groups can fill in the blanks together and share what they wrote. For example, students can come up with questions concerning each peritext type to fill in the Consider column of the table. In addition, students can share their project sheet responses with the class. As a formative assessment, such sharing can enable the teacher to recognize whether students correctly understand the concepts and then use that information to guide students' learning activities in a subsequent class. Once students fully understand peritext, it would be more important to facilitate a discussion about the messages each peritextual element conveys, as well as the article itself.

Dealing with all four peritext types can help students better understand the news article by considering various implications of different elements in the news article. However, teachers can have students focus on only a certain type of peritext according to the learning objectives and the time needed for effective learning.

The application of peritextual elements in online news articles is not limited to high school English classes; it can be contextualized for any other K–12 classes as well as for the school library where a school librarian teaches or collaborates with other teachers. These elements can facilitate reading subject-related news articles and discussions of certain topics. The pilot class did not intend to examine whether the peritext works differently according to topics of news articles or other variables, but this aspect can be tested in various contexts.

## Conclusion

The modified Peritextual Literacy Framework for online news articles offers a new approach to news literacy education. The value of the framework is to provide both an analytical tool and a pedagogical tool. As an analytical tool, the PLF allows for identifying elements found in online news articles according to peritext types. As a pedagogical tool that can be easily used, it supports teaching and learning in the areas of news literacy and information literacy that can contribute to enhancing students' critical thinking skills.

## NOTES

1. Hunt Allcott and Matthew Gentzkow, "Social Media and Fake News in the 2016 Election," *Journal of Economic Perspectives* 31, no. 2 (2017): 213.

2. Reuters Institute for the Study of Journalism, "Reuters Institute Digital News Report 2017" (2017), https://reutersinstitute.politics.ox.ac.uk/sites/default/files/Digital%20News%20Report%202017%20web_0.pdf; Jeffrey Gottfried and Elisa Shearer, "News Use across Social Media Platforms 2016," Pew Research Center (May 26, 2016), www.journalism.org/2016/05/26/news-use-across-social-media-platforms-2016/.

3. American Press Institute and Associated Press-NORC Center for Public Affairs Research, "How Millennials Get News: Inside the Habits of America's First Digital Generation," March 16, 2015, https://www.americanpressinstitute.org/publications/reports/survey-research/millennials-news/.

4. Clifford Christians et al., *Normative Theories of the Media: Journalism in Democratic Societies* (Urbana: University of Illinois Press, 2009); Michael Schudson, Why Democracies Need an Unlovable Press (Cambridge: Polity Press, 2008).

5. Howard Schneider, "It's the Audience, Stupid!," *Nieman Reports* 61, no. 3 (2017).

6. Stony Brook University School of Journalism, Center for News Literacy, *What Is News Literacy?*, www.centerfornewsliteracy.org/what-is-news-literacy.

7. National Council of Teachers of English, *NCTE Position Statement: Resolution on Composing with Nonprint Media* (November 30, 2003), www2.ncte.org/statement/composewithnonprint.

8. BBC, "School Report," www.bbc.co.uk/schoolreport.

9. Renee Hobbs, "News Literacy: What Works and What Doesn't" (paper presented at the Association for Education in Journalism and Mass Communication [AEJMC] Conference, Denver, Colorado, August 7, 2010).

10. BBC, "BBC to Help Students Identify 'Fake News,'" December 6, 2017, www.bbc.com/news/entertainment-arts-42242630.

11. The News Literacy Project, www.thenewsliteracyproject.org; Stony Brook University School of Journalism, *What Is News Literacy?*

12. Partnership for 21st Century Learning, *Framework for 21st Century Learning*, www.p21.0rg/about-us/p21-framework.

13. Partnership for 21st Century Learning, *Framework for 21st Century Learning*.

14. Renee Hobbs, "Building Citizenship Skills through Media Literacy Education," in *The Public Voice in a Democracy at Risk*, ed. Michael Salvador and Patricia and M. Sias (Westport, CT: Greenwood 1998); Renee Hobbs and Richard Frost, "Measuring the Acquisition of Media-Literacy Skills," *Reading Research Quarterly* 38, no. 3 (2003).

15. Schneider, "It's the Audience, Stupid!"; Hobbs, "News Literacy."

16. Hobbs, "News Literacy," 3.

17. Hobbs, "News Literacy," 4.

18. Melissa Gross and Don Latham, "The Peritextual Literacy Framework: Using the Functions of Peritext to Support Critical Thinking," *Library and Information Science Research* 39, no. 2 (2017): 116.

19. Gross and Latham, "The Peritextual Literacy Framework."

20. Emily K. Vraga, Melissa Tully, and Rojas Hernando, "Media Literacy Training Reduces Perception of Bias," *News Research Journal* 30, no. 40 (2009).

21. Jennifer Fleming, "Media Literacy, News Literacy, or News Appreciation? A Case Study of the News Literacy Program at Stony Brook University," *Journalism and Mass Communication Educator* 69, no. 2 (2014): 154.

22. Stanford History Education Group, *Evaluating Information: The Cornerstone of Civic Online Reasoning* (2016), https://stacks.stanford.edu/file/druid:fv751 yt5934/SHEG%20Evaluating%20Information%20Online.pdf.

23. Gérard Genette, *Paratexts: Thresholds of Interpretation* (New York: Cambridge University Press, 1997); Gross and Latham, "The Peritextual Literacy Framework."

24. Genette, *Paratexts*.

25. Dorothee Birke and Birte Christ, "Paratext and Digitized Narrative," *Narrative* 21, no. 1 (2013).

26. American Press Institute and Associated Press-NORC Center for Public Affairs Research, "A New Understanding: What Makes People Trust and Rely on News," (2016).

27. Paul Bradshaw, *The Online Journalism Handbook* (London: Routledge, 2010), https://doi.org/10.4324/9781315834184.

28. Bradshaw, *The Online Journalism Handbook*, 41.

29. Bradshaw, *The Online Journalism Handbook*, 41.

30. Gross and Latham, "The Peritextual Literacy Framework."

31. Gross and Latham, "The Peritextual Literacy Framework."

32. Gross and Latham, "The Peritextual Literacy Framework."

33. Gross and Latham, "The Peritextual Literacy Framework."

34. Gross and Latham, "The Peritextual Literacy Framework."

35. Gross and Latham, "The Peritextual Literacy Framework."

36. Gross and Latham, "The Peritextual Literacy Framework."

37. Alan Blinder, Patricia Mazzei, and Jess Bidgood, "'Bomb Cyclone': Snow and Bitter Cold Blast the Northeast," *New York Times*, January 4, 2018, https://goo.gl/BmKSbQ.

38. BBC News, "Trump: Michael Wolff Book on Administration Is 'Full of Lies,'" January 5, 2018, www.bbc.com/news/world-us-canada-42574419.

# Peritextual Elements in Online News Articles

## (Adapted from the Peritextual Literacy Framework)

| Peritext type | Peritextual elements | Consider |
|---|---|---|
| **Production**<br>(Elements that uniquely identify a work) | Headline<br>Byline: Date, time, writer<br>News provider/ Press agency/ News aggregator | • What do these elements tell you about the work you have in hand?<br>• Where do we find these elements?<br>• What uses are there for these elements?<br>• How do these elements affect your viewpoint about the article?<br>• Does the headline include the whole story and provide the context?<br>• Is the content sponsored or is it the real news story? (Stanford History Education Group, 2016) |
| **Promotional**<br>(Elements that interface between the work and its potential audience) | Author biography<br>Author website URL (link to author's social media accounts)<br>Blurb/bla-bla | • Are these elements present?<br>• How do these elements affect your view of the work?<br>• Are they interesting? Convincing? Effective? |

| Supplemental (Elements outside the text proper that augment understanding of the content) | Still images<br>Audio<br>Video<br>Tables<br>Time line<br>Charts<br>Comments | • How do these help you understand the work better?<br>• Are there elements missing that you wish were there?<br>• How do these elements help the author make his or her points?<br>• Do those elements match the content of the text?<br>• Are those elements proper for the article? |
|---|---|---|
| Documentary (Elements that connect the audience to external works used in the production of the work or that reify or extend the content of the work) | Hyperlinks<br>Image credits (Captions)<br>Source notes<br>Related coverage/ Related articles | • Is it clear where the information came from?<br>• Do these elements help you understand the author's point of view?<br>• Do these elements color your impression of the text?<br>• Is the article based on credible sources?<br>• Are the sources fact-checked?<br>• Do the sources help you to verify the story? |

# Project Sheet

**Day 1: "'Bomb Cyclone': Snow and Bitter Cold Blast the Northeast"**
https://www.nytimes.com/2018/01/04/us/winter-snow-bomb-cyclone
.html?&moduleDetail=section-news-3&action=click&contentCollection=
U.S.&region=Footer&module=MoreInSection&version=WhatsNext&
contentID=WhatsNext&pgtype=article

Shortened URL: https://goo.gl/BmKSbQ

**Day 2: "Trump: Michael Wolff Book on Administration Is 'Full of Lies'"**
www.bbc.com/news/world-us-canada-42574419

- Please skim the news article online.
- What are the peritextual elements you see from the article (e.g., headline, pictures, authors, etc.)?

## Production Peritext
1. What are the production peritextual elements in the article?
2. What do the production peritextual elements tell you?
3. Is production peritext helpful to better understand the news article? Why or why not?

## Promotional Peritext
1. What are the promotional peritextual elements in the article?
2. What do the promotional peritextual elements tell you?
3. Is promotional peritext helpful to better understand the news article? Why or why not?

## Supplemental Peritext

1. What are the supplemental peritextual elements in the article?
2. What do the supplemental peritextual elements tell you?
3. Is supplemental peritext helpful to better understand the news article? Why or why not?

## Documentary Peritext

1. What are the documentary peritextual elements in the article?
2. What do the documentary peritextual elements tell you?
3. Is documentary peritext helpful to better understand the news article? Why or why not?

Do you think peritextual elements in online news articles help you to better understand your online news reading? Why or why not?

$$\bigodot_{11}$$

# (Re)Covering Disney

## Media Peritexts and Media Literacy in the Classroom

PETER C. KUNZE

A COMMON LESSON OF CHILDHOOD IS "DON'T JUDGE A BOOK BY ITS COVER." The aphorism implies, of course, that looks can be deceiving: the new, shy class-mate may soon become a best friend, and the odd-looking and unfamiliar food may turn out to be delicious. Nevertheless, when it actually comes to reading books, judging a book by its cover is not only important, it is encouraged. Net-works of stakeholders—authors, illustrators, designers, marketing experts, and publishing executives—have collaborated to craft that book, and the way in which it is covered answers a range of questions for the potential reader or consumer, including the book's genre, tone, and intended audience.

Notice, for example, how publishers provide well-established books with a new cover to make them appealing to a younger generation of readers. A black-and-white photograph of a brooding teenager in a leather jacket graces the 2006 Speak edition of S. E. Hinton's *The Outsiders* (1967), while the cover of Simon Pulse's 2010 reissue of Maureen Daly's *Seventeenth Summer* uses a recent photograph of two teenagers with their legs intertwined, sitting on a dock over-looking a lake.[1] The title of the book, originally published in 1942, is written in a lime-green script similar to a teenager's handwriting. Atheneum Books' 2014 paperback edition of Judy Blume's *Are You There, God? It's Me, Margaret* features a cover design in which the book's interrogative title is rendered as two text messages from Margaret.[2] A third text message, presumably from God, includes the familiar ellipsis that indicates that someone is typing a response. Blume's classic novel, of course, features no text messaging or even cell phones. After all, the book is over forty years old and predates texting by more than two decades. But the new cover proposes to the reader that this book speaks to enduring concerns for preteens, despite the anachronistic cover design. The feeling of loneliness and the desire for connection suggested by the cover prepare the reader for the content therein and, presumably, entice readers feeling much the same way that this book is for them.

## Theory and Methodology

Book covers are classic examples of what literary theorist Gérard Genette calls "paratexts," supplemental materials beyond the text itself that nevertheless help to frame our reading and, therefore, interpretation of the literary work. In Genette's words, these materials, which may include illustrations, acknowledgment pages, prefaces, indexes, or even promotional materials, function "to make present, to ensure the text's presence in the world, its 'reception' and consumption in the form (nowadays, at least) of a book."[3] Genette distinguishes "epitexts," which are beyond the physical book itself and include interviews with the author or book reviews in a newspaper, from what he terms "peritexts," or those materials that appear within the physical book and that might consist of a foreword or a glossary, for example. These materials, collectively speaking, help to draw in readers, shape their experiences with the text, and potentially influence the meaning they make with it. In short, you can judge a book by its cover—in fact, quite often the publisher wants you to do just that.

With this presumption in mind, Melissa Gross and Don Latham have offered a pedagogical model, the Peritextual Literacy Framework (PLF), for librarians, teachers, and readers to employ while studying a text. Gross and Latham divide peritexts into six functions—production, promotional, intratextual, navigational, supplemental, and documentary—by which students can interrogate how these essential supplements operate within a text. As Gross and Latham explain, the PLF has value in research and teaching across a wide variety of media as it can:

- Reveal the scope of a work and the user's decision as to whether to engage with the work (or not)
- Prepare the user to understand and appreciate the work
- Expose the extent to which a work provides navigational aids and the relative ease with which information contained in the work can be accessed
- Provide insight into the information and sources a work provides without an in-depth analysis of the work itself, allowing users to make a preliminary assessment of the credibility of a work
- Explain how the author knows what the author knows
- Explain what the author is trying to convey
- Clarify understanding of how sources are used in specific disciplines[4]

The framework triangulates the exchange that takes place between the author, the text, and the reader in generating meaning while reading. Although this approach generally works well with books, the very nature of recorded media resists such easy application of this model. This chapter aims to propose a revision when considering film and television texts in particular, acknowledging in the process the fundamental differences in how the texts are produced and consumed.

## Authorship in Media Texts

Authorship has long been a point of contention in the humanities. The myth of singular authorship has been increasingly challenged in studies of children's literature by scholars who have recuperated histories of collaborative authorship with children, as seen in important scholarship by Marah Gubar and Victoria Ford Smith.[5] In media studies, critics and scholars alike resisted literary studies' authorship model from the earliest introduction of the auteur theory in the 1960s. By the 1980s, scholars David Bordwell, Kristin Thompson, Janet Staiger, and Thomas Schatz had shown quite effectively that the studio system itself had had a greater influence in shaping classical Hollywood cinema than had any single job title within it, such as producer or director.[6] Media authorship is always already collaborative, and when it takes place in an industrial context, as it most often does, isolating individual agents for the purposes of "reading" a film or television episode becomes wholly fraught, if not impossible. Although it is true that some directors or producers are treated like "authors" for their creative genius, they still depend on a team of screenwriters, editors, cinematographers, performers, composers, musicians, and so on to execute their vision. In fact, many studios work to erase the individual contributions made to their films in the name of branding or house style.

Perhaps no studio is a greater exemplar of this practice than Disney. Nearing a century of existence, Disney manages to maintain a recognizable style without allowing a single contributor to take creative credit. For example, students can undoubtedly name a range of Disney films, but how often can they name the directors or the screenwriters? Walt Disney, the company's namesake, surely became a mascot for his company alongside his trademark creation, Mickey Mouse, but Walt was a producer. Though he directed many of his early cartoon shorts, his features, by and large, were written and directed by those artists under his direct supervision. (In fact, Mickey himself was designed by Ub Iwerks.) My point here is that the concept of the author does not quite work in the same way for interpreting recorded media as it works for print media. Because authorship requires cooperation in film and television, we need to replace *author* with *studio, production company,* or *industry.*

Media studies scholar Jonathan Gray does just that, proposing a "triumvirate" of Text, Audience, and Industry in his influential study of media paratexts.[7] This approach reminds us that authorship does not lie within a single individual but in a network of agents that have varying degrees of creative power and input. Although this reality persists in media making, very often books include the unacknowledged labor of the writer's trusted readers and assistants, editors, and publishing executives. It can be hard to determine the range of influences without archival work or in-depth interviews, but we can pull back and examine the effect that media producers, even publishers, were trying to create for audiences through the arrangement of elements.

In what follows, I apply the PLF in a slightly augmented form—privileging Disney as a media conglomerate over any single author—to show how this framework may be usefully applied to the study of film with students. As a media studies scholar who also holds a PhD in literary studies, I believe that this discipline can enrich and complement how we teach students to interpret media. Although literary models are often employed in media analysis, I argue that in fact we have to adjust slightly for media texts, which are produced in often different industrial conditions. Focusing on how Disney packages its films for release on DVD, I hope to show the various roles that DVD covers play not only in shaping how one understands the film but also in how one understands Disney itself.

## A Brief History of Disney and Disney Branding

Disney stands as perhaps the most formidable brand in American entertainment. The company began independently producing cartoon shorts in the 1920s, and despite the blockbuster success of its first feature, *Snow White and the Seven Dwarfs*, the company struggled financially through most of the 1930s and 1940s.[8] In the 1950s, Disney found stability as it moved into television in order to secure funding for Disneyland, and the theme parks kept the company afloat through a very difficult creative period lasting from the death of Walt Disney in 1966 through the releases of *Who Framed Roger Rabbit* and *The Little Mermaid*.[9] Under the leadership of Michael Eisner, Frank Wells, and Jeffrey Katzenberg, Disney experienced a veritable "renaissance" that reestablished it as the foremost producer of family entertainment. In the 1990s, while major international conglomerates acquired Hollywood studios, Disney avoided a buyout by becoming a conglomerate in its own right. Over the past fifteen years, Disney has purchased the Muppets, Pixar, Lucasfilm, and Marvel and has initiated efforts to acquire 20th Century Fox. Today, Disney remains the most profitable, the most influential, and the most powerful entertainment company in the United States, and much of its attention continues to focus on children's media.

Part of Disney's recovery in the 1980s can be credited to its expansion into the home video market. Although some studios remained reticent to release their films for consumer purchase, Disney cautiously experimented with releasing compilations of its cartoon shorts ("Silly Symphonies"), the lesser known animated features, and then the legacy films. Through the 1990s and into the 2000s, the company regularly advertised the films as properties from the "Disney Vault," encouraging viewers to purchase them soon before they would be withdrawn from circulation. This practice, commonly referred to in economics as the scarcity principle, spikes sales because people feel that the availability will dwindle and access will be denied. Because Disney films were often released on a limited basis and in elaborate packaging, Disney was conscientiously marketing them as prestige products, especially in comparison to animation produced by its competitors. These strategies provide an opportunity for us to explore questions of persuasion, cultural value, and critical consumerism with our students.

My contention here is that Disney very often uses peritexts to reinforce its own version of its history and, by extension, its branding. Disney is very much a legacy brand. A good deal of its claim to being a family-friendly entertainment company rests in the values of its founder, its tradition of time-honored classics, and its commitments to its artistic style and values despite changing social mores. Of course, these traits are not steadfast: many Disney "classics," such as *Fantasia* or *Pinocchio*, were failures upon initial release, while one clearly sees in *Beauty and the Beast* and *Frozen* attempts to "update" the princesses for today's gender politics.[10] (Many feminist scholars, of course, still dismiss these princesses as sexist representations of femininity, while some go even further by suggesting that the characters have a detrimental effect on young women.)

These tendencies are why paying attention to Disney's DVD covers is important: often, there is a noticeable amount of writing—and rewriting—of the company's own history. For example, following the release of the sequel *Tron: Legacy*, Disney re-released Steven Lisberger's 1982 *Tron* on DVD in 2011.[11] Underneath the film's title on the DVD cover, "The Original Classic" appears in bold lettering, even though the film was roundly dismissed by critics and audiences alike upon initial release. Such historical realities are irrelevant for marketing purposes. The film gained respect among a select group of fans after its release, perhaps justifying Disney's revisionist take on its own history. Similarly, during Disney's "renaissance," the executives put little faith in the animation division, preferring to focus their energies on live-action filmmaking and television production instead. The animated films far exceeded expectations, appealing across age groups and reinvigorating interest in Disney feature animation. They also proved far more profitable for Disney, because animated films could inspire toys, merchandise, books, clothing, and direct-to-video sequels. Therefore, the DVD covers of the films from this period demonstrate not only a pride in these films as aesthetic and cultural texts but also a conscientious attempt to craft a very deliberate history of Disney as a prestigious producer of such texts. Although the history of Disney as a company may seem irrelevant to the concerns of the average classroom, this arguably misleading practice on the company's part provides a valuable opportunity to discuss historiography, prestige, and canons with our students.

## The Peritextual Literacy Framework and Disney DVDs

As previously mentioned, the Peritextual Literacy Framework divides peritexts into six separate functions: production, promotional, navigational, intratextual, supplemental, and documentary. Covers, whether on books or DVDs, serve both production and promotional purposes in our understanding of the texts. Production elements relate to the creation of the work, often allowing the reader to determine who published, produced, wrote, directed, edited, or illustrated the text.[12] These factors are also crucial to both identifying and assessing the work. Promotional elements largely serve a commercial function. They serve to convince the reader or consumer that the text deserves his attention.[13] Attention to the production and promotional aspects of peritexts encourages readers and viewers to understand themselves interchangeably as critics, evaluators, consumers, and meaning makers. For the purposes of this discussion, I want to foreground how the DVD covers implicitly answer the following questions:

- What is the name of the film?
- Who is responsible for the film?
- Why is the film worth the viewer's time?
- How is quality signified to the reader?

Examining DVD covers reveals how Disney packages its films to conceal these processes at work, further underscoring the need for teachers to prepare students to decode these marketing strategies. Luckily, teachers can either closely examine credits with students (on the package or at the end of the film), listen to DVD commentary tracks, or supervise Internet research to retrieve these obscured histories. Preparing students to face these questions encourages them to become more discerning readers, viewers, and consumers.

I have selected four Disney films to analyze, privileging DVD editions released within the past fifteen years: *Fantasia/Fantasia 2000*, *Oliver and Company*, *The Little Mermaid*, and *Aladdin*.[14] I am including *Fantasia* because it was not originally a success, largely considered Disney's vanity project. *Oliver and Company* was released on the edge of the renaissance, but it is generally not considered a classic of the period, whereas *The Little Mermaid* and *Aladdin* stand as benchmarks in contemporary Disney animation, each grossing over $100 million at the box office and reestablishing Disney's reputation in the film industry.

Collectively, these films demonstrate a variety of approaches that Disney employs to make its films enticing to potential viewers and consumers. Teachers and librarians, therefore, have a valuable opportunity to talk about marketing and persuasion through questions such as "What catches your attention here?" and "What can you guess about this movie based on how it is packaged?"

Even today, *Fantasia* stands as a fairly risky endeavor in moviemaking. Rather than a linear narrative, it uses vignettes with brief introductions between segments. Music, not narration, tells the story of each segment, so though it is visually appealing, it can be narratively confusing for some viewers. Despite its poor box office performance, the film has built a reputation over the years. The 2010 DVD release combined *Fantasia* with its "sequel," *Fantasia 2000*, which also fared poorly and perhaps remains most well known for including *Destino*, the recently completed short that began as a collaboration between Walt Disney and Surrealist painter Salvador Dalí. The film's titles are written in slightly different fonts, with Disney's signature above them. Though Disney obviously did not supervise the production of the latter film, his name is synonymous with his brand, and his signature, in particular, continues to be used to reinforce that brand. In fact, the case also includes a quotation from Disney: "FANTASIA is Timeless." Noticeably, this sentiment comes not from a scholar or a critic but from the film's creator, a self-interested tastemaker whom viewers will undoubtedly recognize. Aside from Disney, no one is given credit for creating the film; the consumer has no sense of who wrote, animated, directed, or edited *Fantasia*, because in the Disney model, these are irrelevant to the final product. Also, practically speaking, when people begin to recognize talent, talent can begin to demand more money. Studios such as Disney benefit enormously from deemphasizing the creative contribution of individual artists.

In addition to the popular characters Mickey Mouse and Donald Duck, the cover features whales, satyrs, and a dancing hippopotamus. This balance of familiar faces and exciting new participants testifies to the adventure therein, while the giant cloud behind these characters suggests a certain mystique and grandeur. In fact, the prominence of Mickey Mouse on the cover testifies to Disney's rehistoricizing. In the 1940s, Donald Duck was by far Disney's most popular character, while Mickey's popularity had waned considerably, and Walt Disney was hoping to stage a comeback.[15] A gold ribbon across the top of the case says "2-Disc Special Edition," no doubt an effort to combine two films that do not sell as well individually. In addition to this banner, the shiny cover features raised illustrations. This relief effect sets these DVD cases apart from ordinary packaging while underscoring the film's worthiness of children's attention. The high production value also suggests the prestige of Disney films without discussing content. Teachers and librarians could compare Disney DVD covers to the cover for an animated film not produced by Disney to notice how prestige and quality are coded for consumers.

This packaging contrasts significantly with the cover of the 2009 *Oliver and Company* DVD, which includes neither the relief nor the shiny exterior. The cover features only the Disney signature, the title, and a "20th Anniversary Edition" banner. As mentioned, *Oliver and Company* came out of a period when Disney was less invested in feature animation, and the film achieved modest success at the box office. The film's animation style is noticeably rougher than later Disney animated features, with harsh lines and more naturalistic coloring. The film places Oliver and his mentor, Dodger, at the center, with supporting characters on the periphery staring at them. The characters, grinning and upbeat, are in an alley, with the New York City skyline in the background. The cover plays up the film's claim to the adventure genre, an action-packed alternative to the traditional Disney princess narrative. What is striking, though, is how unremarkable the packaging is. Clearly, Disney has less confidence in the film to sell on DVD, and it is priced lower than other Disney films. Teachers and librarians might consult websites such as Amazon and Barnes and Noble with students to see how these websites promote the film compared to the packaging. Because it does not have prestigious credentials to fall back on, the amount of bonus materials included with *Oliver and Company* does not come close to the wealth of featurettes included with subsequent Disney films of this period, especially *Beauty and the Beast* and the movies discussed later in this chapter.

The 2006 DVD release of *The Little Mermaid*, however, is billed as the Platinum Edition. It contains two DVDs, including games, activities, cartoon shorts, deleted scenes, advertisements for theme park ride tie-ins, and behind-the-scenes materials. No one receives credit for creating the film; only the requisite Walt Disney signature is evident. The film's worth is conveyed through the large image of Ariel on the cover, with the supporting characters—Ursula, Flounder,

Sebastian, and Titan—surrounding her. Her suitor, Prince Eric, is conspicuously missing, but his ship appears in the top corner, making a claim for the film's adventure credentials. This inclusion speaks to the presumed interests of boys—a sea tale—over girls, who presumably want a princess romance narrative. Like *Fantasia*, the film uses a relieved, shiny cover. This film, unlike *Oliver and Company*, represents the best of Disney's efforts, warranting an elaborate edition to underscore its canonicity in both Disney animation and Hollywood cinema.

Unlike earlier Disney films, *Aladdin* focuses on a prince rather than a princess. Yet, the 2004 DVD release, the Platinum Edition (in a silver banner across the top), more prominently features the Genie, Aladdin's faithful sidekick famously performed by Robin Williams. The title is stylized in the center, with the signature above and "2-Disc Special Edition" below. Although no one receives creative credit on the cover, the DVD was available in a larger Collector's Edition packaging that included a DVD companion book and character portrait drawings featuring animator signatures. In feature animation at Disney, one or two animators are usually assigned to each character to conceive and standardize the animation. These drawings feature the signature of the individual animator, a rare opportunity for fans to learn the names of the individual animators without combing film credits or the Internet. Of course, this acknowledgment of creative contribution was not directly used in marketing the DVD. The bottom half of the cover features Aladdin and Jasmine on the magic carpet, with Abu comically hanging on, while the villainous Jafar shakes his fist as his parrot Iago squawks in the opposing corner. The cover masterfully presents the film's genres: comedy (the Genie, Abu, and Iago), adventure (Jafar, the magic carpet, the cave), and romance (Aladdin and Jasmine).

In my own classroom, I will often show students movie posters so that they can determine the genre through various elements, including the use of color, fonts, character poses, and graphics. Drawing students' attention to these subtle codes and guiding them through analysis prepare them to transfer those skills into nonclassroom contexts, such as watching television or seeing a billboard. Although this film allegedly targeted boys, the packaging of the DVD indicates that Aladdin clearly aims to appeal to traditional expectations of both genders. The cover also opens to reveal a detailed breakdown of the bonus materials, including music videos, "making of" featurettes, deleted scenes, games, and sing-alongs. The hours of additional activities speak to a confidence in Aladdin as a Disney product and a desire to showcase it for future generations.

## Conclusion

The energy committed to *Fantasia*, *The Little Mermaid*, and *Aladdin* demonstrates Disney's attempt to write—and rewrite—its own history. The most ambitious and well-received films are lauded, while seemingly minimal efforts are afforded to the film that had lower production values and that was less financially and critically successful. In turn, this initiative directs more attention and more dollars to the more well-packaged films, reinforcing notions of Disney's quality and revising its complicated reception history of monumental successes and just-as-impressive failures. Future research might examine the bonus materials themselves, especially the "making of" featurettes and the audio commentaries, which can be turned on or off while viewing. These optional peritexts are fascinating not only in how they influence viewing but in how they speak to the presumed audiences for Disney films. As a classroom activity, teachers and librarians could discuss whether and how students can maintain dual focus on the commentaries and the film as well as how one alternately informs our understanding of the other.

Just as teachers use biographical information about authors to teach books, teaching films may require research into the history of production companies, studios, or the media industries in general. Numerous books, websites, documentaries, and YouTube videos do this work already, and teachers and librarians can easily integrate them into their classrooms. Although this task may seem laborious, the payoffs would be considerable. First, it demonstrates to students how different media demand learning new hermeneutical approaches or adapting extant models from literary criticism. Second, it allows instructors to explore with students the malleable, politicized, and narrativized nature of history: how it is created, shaped, and revised. Finally, the development of media-literacy skills can transfer not only into how students examine advertisements, television, and other films but also into their decisions about how they spend their money. As a result, critical media literacy, assisted by the PLF, potentially has long-lasting effects, helping us to prepare our students to be stronger readers, viewers, consumers, and citizens.

## NOTES

1.  S. E. Hinton, *The Outsiders* (New York: Speak, 2006); Maureen Daly, *Seventeenth Summer* (New York: Simon Pulse, 2010).

2.  Judy Blume, *Are You There, God? It's Me, Margaret* (New York: Atheneum Books for Young Readers, 2014).

3.  Gérard Genette, *Paratexts: Thresholds of Interpretation,* trans. Jane E. Lewin (New York: Cambridge University Press, 1997), 1.

4.  Melissa Gross and Don Latham, "The Peritextual Literacy Framework: Using the Functions of Peritext to Support Critical Thinking," *Library and Information Science Research* 39, no. 2 (2017): 118–19.

5.  Marah Gubar, *Artful Dodgers: Reconceiving the Golden Age of Children's Literature* (New York: Oxford University Press, 2009); Victoria Ford Smith, *Between Generations: Collaborative Authorship in the Golden Age of Children's Literature* (Jackson: University Press of Mississippi, 2017).

6.  See David Bordwell, Kristin Thompson, and Janet Staiger, *The Classical Hollywood Cinema: Film Style and Mode of Production to 1960* (New York: Columbia University Press, 1985); Thomas Schatz, *The Genius of the System: Hollywood Filmmaking in the Studio Era* (New York: Pantheon, 1990).

7.  Jonathan Gray, *Show Sold Separately: Promos, Spoilers, and Other Media Paratexts* (New York: New York University Press, 2010), 23.

8.  Walt Disney, David Hand, Adriana Caselotti, Harry Stockwell, Lucille La Verne, Moroni Olsen, Ted Sears, et al., *Snow White and the Seven Dwarfs* (Burbank, CA: Walt Disney Enterprises, 2001).

9.  Ron Clements, John Musker, Jodi Benson, René Auberjonois, and Christopher Daniel Barnes, *The Little Mermaid* (2016); Robert Zemeckis, Jeffrey Price, Peter S. Seaman, Robert Watts, Frank Marshall, Bob Hoskins, Charles Fleischer, et al., *Who Framed Roger Rabbit* (2016), https://www.swank.com.

10. Walt Disney Productions and Deems Taylor, *Walt Disney's Fantasia: In Technicolor and Fantasound* (New York: Walt Disney Productions, 1940); Campbell Grant, *Walt Disney's Pinocchio* (New York: Simon and Schuster, 1948); Alan Menken and Howard Ashman, *Walt Disney Pictures Presents Beauty and the Beast* (Milwaukee, WI: H. Leonard, 1991); Walt Disney Animation Studios, *Frozen,* directed by Chris Buck and Jennifer Lee, produced by Peter Del Vecho, screenplay by Jennifer Lee (Burbank, CA: Walt Disney Studios Home Entertainment, 2014).

11. Joseph Kosinski, Eddy Kitsis, Adam Horowitz, Jeff Bridges, Garrett Hedlund, Olivia Wilde, Bruce Boxleitner, Michael Sheen, Steven Lisberger, and Bonnie MacBird, *Tron: Legacy* ([Burbank, CA]: Walt Disney Studios Home Entertainment, 2011); Jeff Bridges, Bruce Boxleitner, Garrett Hedlund, and Olivia Wilde, *Tron: Legacy* ([Burbank, CA]: Disney, 2010), DVD.

12. Gross and Latham, "The Peritextual Literacy Framework," 119.

13. Shelbie Witte, Melissa Gross, and Don Latham, "Using the Peritextual Literacy Framework with Young Adult Biographies: Introducing Peritextual Functions with Adolescents in Social Studies," in *Adolescent Literature as a Complement to*

*the Content Areas: Social Sciences and the Humanities*, ed. Paula Greathouse, Joan F. Kaywell, and Brooke Eisenbach (Lanham, MD: Rowman and Littlefield, 2017), 72.

14. Ben Sharpsteen, Walt Disney, Donald W. Ernst, James Levine, Steve Martin, Leopold Stokowski, Ralph Grierson, and Kathleen Battle, *Fantasia: Fantasia 2000* (Burbank, CA: Walt Disney Studios Home Entertainment, 2010); Dom DeLuise, Joey L., and Cheech Marin, *Oliver and Company 20th* ([Burbank, CA]: Disney, 2009); Ron Clements, John Musker, René Auberjonois, Jodi Benson, Pat Carroll, and H. C. Andersen, *The Little Mermaid* (Burbank, CA: Walt Disney Home Entertainment, 2006); Alan Menken, Howard Ashman, Tim Rice, Ron Clements, John Musker, Ted Elliott, Terry Rossio, et al., *Aladdin* (Burbank, CA: Walt Disney, 2004).

15. Susan Ohmer, "Laughter by Numbers: The Science of Comedy at the Walt Disney Studio," in *Funny Pictures: Animation and Comedy in Studio-Era Hollywood,* ed. Daniel Goldmark and Charlie Keil (Berkeley: University of California, 2011), 116.

# Leading Students to Exit through the Gift Shop:

## Reading Banksy's Public Art through Documentary Film and Director's Cuts

JENNIFER S. DAIL, W. KYLE JONES, AND GLENN CHANCE

LIKE PRINT-BASED TEXTS, FILMS AND OTHER DEFINED DIGITAL MEDIA HAVE their own peritextual (outside the text proper) and epitextual (outside the text) elements that support viewers in accessing, evaluating, and comprehending the content.[1] Good documentary films have several defining characteristics with regard to both the story and the filmmaking process.[2] The stories in documentary films focus on people who wield power and influence events and information, which is the focus of Banksy's own graffiti grounded in political activism. These stories also raise more questions than they answer, which plays into the myth surrounding Banksy and his identity. The filmmaking process focuses on several elements of the text proper. In terms of these elements, documentary films use a mix of live-action shots and still shots to serve as transitions between live-action scenes; the images of still shots bring credibility to the film through their relevance to people, information, or places. The soundtrack is another textual element of documentary film because it sets the tone. Documentary and other films use paratextual elements as well. DVD releases of films may contain a director's cut (peritext) to support viewers' understanding of the film and the decisions contributing to its final composition. Epitextual elements of films are broad ranging, including reviews, critical analyses, supporting websites, and director and actor interviews.

This chapter examines student-created films functioning as epitext in response to the documentary film *Exit through the Gift Shop*.[3] Based on Banksy, an anonymous graffiti street artist who often uses his work for political activism, *Exit through the Gift Shop* explores and promotes the enigma that surrounds Banksy and the overnight appearance of his graffiti art. The students' epitextual films are based on the peritext in the director's cut, which unpacks the behind-the-scenes thinking of film as text. These epitextual films present a critical response to the original film as students analyze the issues presented and relate those issues to their world.

The guerilla style (e.g., home video quality, unsteady camera handling) of Banksy's documentary film serves as a model for the students' director's cuts, encouraging students to embrace the do-it-yourself qualities of *Exit through the Gift Shop* and purposefully asking students to consider the merits of such a style and its impact on their own films. Banksy self-produced his documentary, which begins as a story about a local man in Los Angeles who videotapes everything as a hobby and one day discovers that his cousin is the street artist known as Space Invader. The film quickly navigates the audience through the man's encounters with other street artists and his filming of their exploits across the city, which ultimately leads to his following and filming of Banksy. All the while, an omniscient narrator with a pleasant British accent provides insight into what the audience is witnessing on the screen. The documentary plays up Banksy's mystique, shrouding him in shadows and altering his voice anytime he is speaking on camera, but it also gives a glimpse into how his art "pops up" overnight.

The mystery surrounding Banksy offers immediate intrigue for students, creating an entry point for them in engaging with nonprint texts in the classroom. Student-created director's cuts serve as the primary epitextual element examined in this chapter and are informed by other epitextual elements such as websites, images (remixed and original photos), and short, five-minute documentaries. In exploring Banksy's work through film, students engage in reading the film as text, stretching their critical reading of text beyond print and developing and applying new skills such as reading and analyzing how modes such as an image, sound, and motion work together as a text.

This type of commentary is typically the focus of director's cuts, which often provide peritext that demonstrates how the director unpacked the thinking behind her filmmaking strategies. As the director of his own documentary, Banksy does not offer viewers a director's cut, leaving opportunity for students to critically read the film as text and create their own extension work. Moving outward from reading and discussing the film as text, students then apply critical literacy stances in creating their own digital Banksy pieces. Finally, students create their own peritext by creating a director's commentary with other students. This activity puts the thinking behind their own composition into conversation with the original text. By doing this, students become more aware of an intention about their rhetorical choices in digital composing, adding a reflective metacognitive component to the textual analysis and production.

## Context

The authors of this chapter are a team composed of a university professor (Jennifer Dail), a doctoral candidate (Kyle Jones), and a teacher in his third year of teaching (Glenn Chance). In her role as a university professor, Dail mentors Jones and Chance, visiting their school when she can, and Jones serves as an on-site mentor at the school. This informal mentorship structure creates a system in which we can share and develop ideas and help one another troubleshoot those ideas before and during implementation. This structure has resulted in our being positioned to provide Chance with an outside lens regarding the work in his classroom.

This study was conducted at a high school located in the suburbs of a metropolitan area in the southeastern United States. Opened in 2010, the school is newer than others in its district and serves a diverse community. Demographically, the school is approximately 45 percent Caucasian, 25 percent Hispanic/Latino, 20 percent Black/African American, 6 percent Asian, and 4 percent other and has a free and reduced-price lunch rate of 35 percent. The study included sixty ninth graders in an English language arts class with half of those students labeled as on-level students and the other half labeled as honors or gifted-level students. The classes were demographically similar to the school with 50 percent Caucasian, 23 percent Hispanic/Latino, 20 percent Black/African American, and 7 percent Asian. The students discussed in the following section were a small sample of the entire participant group and include three students labeled as honors or gifted students—Serena, Alexis, and Elodie—and three labeled as on-level students—Essence, Daniel, and Phoebe. All names are pseudonyms to protect the identities of the students.

## Method and Application

*As they enter Mr. Chance's classroom, students pick up a packet on the documentary film* Exit through the Gift Shop *about the enigmatic and anonymous street artist known as Banksy. After completing a short warm-up, Mr. Chance starts the documentary, and students become genuinely riveted by the opening of the film, actively laughing or reacting verbally with surprise as they watch. After twenty minutes have passed, Mr. Chance stops the film when Shepard Fairey, another famous street artist known for his "Obey" art featuring the face of the late André the Giant, says street art gave him "real power from perceived power." Mr. Chance repeats the statement before leading the students through a discussion about what they believe about street art's validity and whether it is vandalism. Students provide dichotomous views of street art with some embracing it as true art, some arguing that it brings about moral concern, and some saying that they like the art but still feel that it is vandalism. One student astutely comments that the difference really has to do with intent, which Mr. Chance relates back to the author's purpose. A few students are upset that street art even happens, with one student wondering, "The mountain of evidence in this documentary, how are these people not in jail?" Mr. Chance compliments the students on how well they are "riffing" off one another and building on one another's comments. The students wrestle with the blurred lines of morality and legality that street art presents for society—"Is it truly art?" "Is it defacing private property?" "Do these artists have a right to express themselves in public spaces?" There is no shortage of raised hands to contribute to the discourse, including one astute student mentioning that "[street art is] not just a moral issue but also an economic concern that could hurt businesses." A student claps and cheers when that student makes her case. Another student brings up concerns about the vulgarity sometimes found in street art and how a young child might not need to see it. The discourse continues as Mr. Chance has the students revisit the opening of the film and consider how the peritextual elements such as title, imagery, shot style, and voiceover inform their perceptions and assumptions about Banksy, street art, and the documentarian himself.*

Exploring visual literacy concepts and using documentary as a means to promote critical thinking and understanding of memoir in the English language arts classroom was the crux of the study as it relates to peritextual analysis. As seen in the preceding vignette, Glenn navigates a critical discussion of a documentary's peritextual elements in order to welcome heightened critical thought during discussion as it relates to documentary as a text. To build to the moment described in the vignette, Glenn spent weeks explicitly teaching visual literacy concepts, using the elements of Hilary Janks's critical visual literacy approach, in order to prepare his students to bridge their recently acquired knowledge of memoir from reading *Tuesdays with Morrie* and *The Last Lecture* with visual literacy and documentary as another medium for biography and autobiography.[4] Ultimately, exploration of both memoir and documentary was used to promote critical thinking and build students' recognition of author purpose or intent.

The Peritextual Literacy Framework (PLF) claims that the value of looking closely at peritextual elements in any text is to prepare users to understand and appreciate a work, explain how the author knows what he knows, and explain what the author is trying to convey, among other potential benefits.[5] Using the lens of the PLF, Glenn designed his unit covering memoir and visual literacy to leverage the street artist Banksy's work and still images as an essential truss of the bridge to critical thinking that he was constructing with his students. In order to move beyond simply identifying visual elements and interpreting them, Glenn had students develop their own digital Banksy-like images with the intent of making those images public and producing their own mini-documentaries about the images they created. The hope was that students would take in peritextual elements, interpret those elements as they aligned with consumed text (e.g., memoirs, photograph collections, and documentary), and apply their own paratextual elements to their images and documentary in an effort to build critical thinking and and to interpret the author's purpose and intent.

The artifacts that students produced varied largely because of the time constraints inevitable in any school environment. Developing students' understanding of visual literacy concepts as a sort of tool kit for student use took weeks to accomplish. Before an image of Banksy's could be critiqued or discussed, let alone before watching a documentary, students had to spend time familiarizing themselves with new terminology (e.g., type of shot, type of angle, gaze, cropping, framing, etc.) as well as learning how to apply those terms to discussing and writing about still and moving images. Although the time spent developing the tool kit for critical visual literacy was essential, it left much less time to create student products, including the documentaries. Essentially, Glenn and most of his students ran out of time to produce work that could truly reflect the potential impact of paratext on their own creations. Still, students did thoroughly discuss and reflect on paratext as seen on websites attributed to Banksy (e.g., the WebQuest used to introduce students to Banksy's work[6]) and the film *Exit through the Gift Shop*. Potentially more important, students produced their own images and made a strong attempt to create a documentary despite the time constraints.

The images that students produced ranged in focus, topic, and purpose. Some paralleled Banksy's intent in his images by taking social justice stances. For example, Serena's and Daniel's pieces focused on the refugee crisis and racism, respectively (figures 12.1 and 12.2). Other students used their images to comment on political issues (e.g., Elodie's focus on global warming and the Environmental Protection Agency; figure 12.3) or immediate, personal concerns (e.g., Essence's focus on bullying, figure 12.4), while still other students focused on personal goals, beliefs, and philosophies (e.g., Alexis's focus on the word Hope in figure 12.5, and Phoebe's focus on achieving the dream of dancing professionally, shown in figure 12.6). Several of the images provide anchor text to help demonstrate the image maker's intent, while others rely on a viewer's familiarity with the imagery to discern intent. No matter the construction, the students produced reflective paragraphs explaining their visual literacy concept choices and the intent of their image for their audience. In tandem with their images and paragraphs, students were to produce a short documentary of approximately three to five minutes showing other students reacting to their piece and their response to that reaction. To do this, students worked in pairs or triads. Although the images and paragraphs were completed by almost every student, students struggled to complete relevant documentaries within the time remaining in the unit. Still, the images and text demonstrate the confluence of visual literacy, traditionally written text, and student images acting as paratext for their documentaries.

The student-produced reflective paragraph explanations of their images convey the importance of pairing image making with traditional text and how the image can act as a peritext for the writing or central content as well as, in this

FIGURE 12.1  **Serena's work**

FIGURE 12.2  **Daniel's work**

FIGURE 12.3  **Elodie's work**

FIGURE 12.4  **Essence's work**

FIGURE 12.6  **Phoebe's work**

FIGURE 12.5  **Alexis's work**

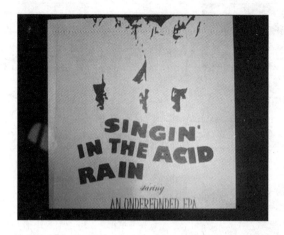

**FIGURE 12.7**

**Opening image of Elodie's director's cut**

case, a documentary. The strongest example of the image acting as peritext was Elodie's opening image of her director's cut (figure 12.7). She used the image she produced as a title screen for her mini-documentary before beginning a voiceover narration of the image. Her image acted as the impetus for the content of her film. In most cases, however, even when students had a title screen, they did not use their own images. Most films began immediately with the camera centered on the students, who would later hold up or share a screenshot of the image they created, ensuring that the image was part of the central content of their director's cut.

The paragraph explanations provided students the opportunity to demonstrate their understanding of an author's purpose while using critical thinking. For instance, Serena, commenting on her image's purpose, wrote, "My image is about immigration. . . . We ignore them as if they were never there to start with. Our selfishness is getting in the way of our humanity," and continued explaining how she created that intent through the use of gaze. She explained, "Gaze is a visual literacy that I used because you can see that the man is looking at the perfect beautiful sky and the other man is looking at the boat. And the way that they are looking is gaze because, one man looks worried or troubled and the other looks relaxed." The implication here is that the gaze (what is being looked at) of the subjects in her image implies both inattention and apathy. Daniel, Essence, and Alexis similarly defined their images' purpose while also explaining how they purposefully used elements of visual literacy in their images. This unpacking of students' own images as they relate to their experiences of unpacking images of street art supports the notion that critical thinking can be developed using a peritextual lens whereby images can act as precursors to expository, argumentative, or narrative text.

Of the six students, only Phoebe and Elodie produced a documentary to complement their image and text. Both students provided a title for their documentaries, but only Elodie's included a credit shot at the end. Elodie's documentary opened with a close-up of her image as she described the image's purpose: "It's addressing how I feel about [how] the public and government ignores issues like global warming and other environmental problems even though they are very important and relevant to all of us." She proceeded to explain the elements of visual literacy that she used, such as a focus on layout and positioning. Phoebe's documentary (figure 12.8) was edited with a consideration for style, using differing shot ranges and using a black-and-white filter throughout. About midway through the documentary, Phoebe explained that her image was "about never giving up on your dreams" and "if you don't think you can do it then you can't, but you can if you put your mind to it." She went on to describe her use of cropping and range in her image.

In both films, a student partner had to provide a critique of the work, and the image maker had the opportunity to respond to the critique. Phoebe's partner stated, "Phoebe's piece is developed because it shows she is passionate about dancing . . . and I think it gives really good detail by [the dancer's] body position," but she goes on to say that ballet dancing is not her style and that she did not personally care for it. Clearly, Phoebe's partner was not critical of the visuals of Phoebe's piece; rather, the student was complimentary, to which Phoebe responded, "[The student's reaction] made me feel fine because she said she liked it and it actually kind of had a purpose," and in response to ballet not being her partner's preferred style of dance, Phoebe said "that saying [her partner's] opinion was more effective because you realize how different

**FIGURE 12.8**
**Phoebe's documentary**

dreams are in the world." Elodie's partner shared, "The title and what's below it is what grabbed me . . . it was pretty straightforward," but also critiqued Elodie's piece, claiming, "You couldn't really see [the actors'] bodies. You could only see their heads and some shadows and their feet." Elodie responded by stating, "The criticism was fair. The filter I used did blur out a lot of the parts of their bodies and made a big massive light with a little black," and she agreed that her piece was meant to be straightforward and that there was "no room for subtlety." The indication in both instances might be that students can not only leverage peritextual elements to better understand texts they consume but also use those elements appropriately in their own texts and products to support more complex academic tasks.

Both documentaries showcase the potential of students looking at multi-modal text through a peritextual lens. One documentary maker saw value in ensuring that there were credits while the other ensured that there was a title screen, music in the background, and an introduction. Again, with more time, students may have produced even stronger documentary products, but the few that were completed demonstrate the layers of complexity that students can extrapolate when moving through various mediums of text, interpreting and creating their own texts with consideration not just of the primary content of the text but of what surrounds and supports that text.

## Conclusion and Recommendations

Although time constraints prove a reality in every classroom, well-supported lessons still help students develop the more discrete critical reading and composing skills we seek as teachers. The scope of this entire project proved too much for most students within the time frame allotted; however, they still learned about peritextual elements and practiced applying them in their own composition process. As a teacher and his supporting mentors, we learned about the background knowledge that students need in order to be successful with this type of work and the time required for building that knowledge. We dare say that this time requirement may be a reason teachers shy away from taking up larger, multimodal composing work in response to critically reading both print and nonprint texts in their classrooms.

Through implementing this project, we saw students develop critical thinking skills in a variety of ways. Students not only consumed a variety of nonprint text types but composed them as well. In doing so, they demonstrated not only an understanding of but also an evaluation and application of visual literacy concepts. Many students demonstrated these skills with visual literacy concepts as well. Finally, before even moving into producing images and director's cuts, students honed their discussion skills by providing strong, evidence-based responses. These results all align with the NCTE/IRA Standards for the English Language Arts:

- *Standard 1:* Students read a wide range of print and nonprint texts to build an understanding of texts, of themselves, and of the cultures of the United States and the world.
- *Standard 3:* Students apply a wide range of strategies to comprehend, interpret, evaluate, and appreciate texts.
- *Standard 5:* Students employ a wide range of strategies as they write and use different writing process elements appropriately to communicate with different audiences for a variety of purposes.
- *Standard 8:* Students use a variety of technological and information resources to gather and synthesize information and to create and communicate knowledge.
- *Standard 11:* Students participate as knowledgeable, reflective, creative, and critical members of a variety of literacy communities.[7]

Based on our experience with this work, we have several recommendations for teachers who want to implement these types of in-depth, across-text readings and response products with students. Because managing time for these sorts of transmedia tasks will typically prove difficult, we suggest embedding elements of visual literacy throughout the course of an instructional year. More specifically, visual literacy skills can be taught over the course of time by using warm-up activities or by using their elements for concluding activities (or doing both) and can connect to almost any unit of study. The idea here is that students will build the tool kit necessary to critically respond to images so that when they get to a unit focusing on analyzing images, they will already be equipped with the requisite tools and terminology. In addition, the unit we shared in this chapter can be simplified and can focus on the documentary and director's cut alone rather than pairing them with a specific artist or static artwork. The use of short documentaries to inspire the creation of student documentaries can save time and, again, can be connected to almost any topic. The most important recommendation is to not go this route alone if possible. Having another educator on board, even if she is a virtual friend at another school, ensures that a teacher has support and access to regular reflection. The high level of reflection that led to making deft moves and pivoting throughout the unit was only possible due to the collaboration between Glenn and Kyle, who discussed almost daily what worked, what did not work, and how to adjust to improve the experience for students in the next class meeting.

## NOTES

1. Melissa Gross and Don Latham, "The Peritextual Literacy Framework: Using the Functions of Peritext to Support Critical Thinking," *Library and Information Science Research* 39, no. 2 (2017): 116–23.

2. Stewart Dunlop, "What Makes a Good Documentary Film? Finding the Story, Assembling the Team, Filming and Editing: What Will Move a Documentary Film to the Ranks of Greatness," last modified 2015, www.documentarytube.com/articles/what-makes-a-good-documentary-film.

3. *Exit through the Gift Shop*, directed by Banksy (London, UK: Revolver Entertainment, 2010), DVD.

4. Hilary Janks, *Doing Digital Literacy: Texts and Activities for Students and Teachers* (New York: Routledge, 2014).

5. Gross and Latham, "The Peritextual Literacy Framework."

6. Kyle Jones and Glenn Chance, "Who Is Banksy?" (2017), www.tinyurl.com/whoisbanksywebquest.

7. National Council of Teachers of English and International Reading Association, "NCTE/IRA Standards for the English Language Arts," last modified November 2012, www.ncte.org/standards/ncte-ira.

# ABOUT THE EDITORS
# AND CONTRIBUTORS

## Editors

**MELISSA GROSS, PhD,** is a professor in the School of Information at Florida State University and a past president of the Association for Library and Information Science Education (ALISE). She received her PhD in Library and Information Science from the University of California, Los Angeles in 1998, received the prestigious American Association of University Women Recognition Award for Emerging Scholars in 2001, and has published extensively in the areas of information-seeking behavior, information literacy, library program and service evaluation, and information resources for youth. Her most recent book is *Five Steps of Outcome-Based Planning and Evaluation for Public Libraries* (ALA Editions, 2016), coauthored with Cindy Mediavilla and Virginia Walter.

**DON LATHAM, PhD,** is a professor in the School of Information at Florida State University. He has served as a board member of the Association for Library and Information Science Education (ALISE), a member of the Young Adult Library Services Association (YALSA) Research Committee and Research Journal Advisory Committee, and chair of the YALSA Excellence in Nonfiction Award Committee. He has published extensively in the areas of information literacy, information behavior of youth, and young adult literature. He is the author of *David Almond: Memory and Magic* (Scarecrow, 2006) and the coauthor along with Melissa Gross of *Young Adult Resources Today: Connecting Teens with Books, Music, Games, Movies, and More* (Rowman and Littlefield, 2014).

**SHELBIE WITTE, PhD,** is the Chuck and Kim Watson Endowed Chair in Education and a professor in Adolescent Literacy and English Education at Oklahoma

State University, where she directs the OSU Writing Project and the Initiative for 21st Century Literacies Research. She serves as coeditor (with Sara Kajder) of *Voices from the Middle*, the premier middle-level journal of the National Council of Teachers of English. Witte has published extensively in the area of 21st century literacies, including *Toward a More Visual Literacy: Shifting the Paradigm with Digital Tools and Young Adult Literature* (Rowman and Littlefield, 2018) and *Young Adult Literature and the Digital World: Textual Engagement through Visual Literacy* (Rowman and Littlefield, 2018), both with Jennifer S. Dail and Steven Bickmore.

## Contributors

**HYERIN BAK** is a doctoral student in the School of Information at Florida State University. She earned her MSLIS degree from Syracuse University. Her research interests focus on information literacy instruction and learning assessment, academic libraries, and learning analytics. She was involved in the pilot study that tested use of the Peritextual Literacy Framework. In that study, she collected and analyzed data from middle school students who applied the framework to an analysis of STEAM texts.

**GLENN CHANCE** is an English teacher at Lanier High School in Sugar Hill, Georgia, where he is heavily involved in project-based learning. His work has been published in *Connections,* the journal of the Georgia Council of Teachers of English. He believes in writing alongside his students and believes that literacy skills and practices happen both on and off the pages they create together.

**SEAN P. CONNORS** is an associate professor of English education at the University of Arkansas. His scholarship and teaching focus on the application of diverse critical perspectives to young adult literature. He has published in a number of scholarly journals and is the editor of *The Politics of Panem: Challenging Genres*, a collection of critical essays about the Hunger Games series.

**JENNIFER S. DAIL** is a professor of English education in the Department of English at Kennesaw State University in the metro-Atlanta area of Georgia.

She also directs the Kennesaw Mountain Writing Project (KMWP), a National Writing Project site serving teachers Pre-K through college in all content areas. Dail served as coeditor of *SIGNAL Journal*, the International Reading Association's journal focusing on young adult literature, from 2008 to 2013. She is also an active member of several educational organizations, including the National Council of Teachers of English (NCTE) and the National Writing Project (NWP). She serves on the board for the Georgia Council of Teachers of English (GCTE) as the college liaison. Dail has published multiple articles on young adult literature and technology in *The ALAN Review* and has written several book chapters focusing on this work as well.

**ERIN DAUGHERTY** is a doctoral candidate in rhetoric, composition, and literacy studies at the University of Arkansas. Her research focuses on the application of socio-spatial and material theories of literacy and how young adults in rural areas can engage in literacy learning by researching and writing about the places they are from.

**LUCIANA C. DE OLIVEIRA, PhD,** is a professor and chair in the Department of Teaching and Learning in the School of Education and Human Development at the University of Miami, Florida. Her research focuses on issues related to teaching English language learners (ELL students) at the K–12 level, including the role of language in learning the content areas, and teacher education, advocacy, and social justice. Prior to coming to UM, de Oliveira served on the faculty of Teachers College, Columbia University. De Oliveira was an elected board member (2013–2016) and currently is president-elect (2017–2018) of the TESOL International Association.

**KEVIN DYKE** is the maps and spatial data curator at the Oklahoma State University Library. He was previously spatial data analyst/curator at the John R. Borchert Map Library at the University of Minnesota. He manages the paper and digital map collections and provides workshops and consultations about web mapping and geographic information systems. One of his chief research interests is the ability of geospatial technology to facilitate historical research and learning.

**ANTERO GARCIA, PhD,** is an assistant professor in the Graduate School of Education at Stanford University where he studies how technology and gaming shape both youth and adult learning, literacy practices, and civic identities. His most recent research studies explore learning and literacies in tabletop role-playing games such as *Dungeons & Dragons* and how participatory culture shifts classroom relationships and instruction. Garcia's research has appeared in numerous journals, including the *Harvard Educational Review*, *Teachers College Record*, and *Reading and Writing Quarterly*. His most recent books are *Good Reception: Teens, Teachers, and Mobile Media in a Los Angeles High School*; *Doing Youth Participatory Action Research: Transforming Inquiry with Researchers, Educators, and Students* (with Nicole Mirra and Ernest Morrell); and *Pose, Wobble, Flow: A Culturally Proactive Approach to Literacy Instruction* (with Cindy O'Donnell-Allen).

**CRAG HILL, PhD,** is Rainbolt Family Endowed Education Presidential Professor and coordinator of English education at the University of Oklahoma. His scholarly work includes two edited collections from Routledge: *Teaching Comics through Multiple Lenses: Critical Perspectives* (2016) and *The Critical Merits of Young Adult Literature: Coming of Age* (2014). He also is the coeditor of an online, open access journal devoted to empirical and critical scholarship on young adult literature, *Study and Scrutiny: Research on Young Adult Literature*.

**BUD HUNT** is the IT and technical services manager for the Clearview Library District in northern Colorado. As an educational consultant and technologist, he explores how to create environments and experiences that support innovative teaching and learning while preserving freedom, choice, and opportunity for all learners across multiple contexts.

**KYLE JONES** is the academy coach at Lanier High School in Sugar Hill, Georgia. His research has focused on participatory culture and identity in the English language arts classroom and, more recently, on visual literacy and project-based learning across curricula. He is a researcher-practitioner who has written articles on personal classroom experiences, project-based learning, and teacher leadership.

**LOREN JONES** is a doctoral candidate specializing in literacy and language learning for English as a second language students in the Department of Teaching and Learning at the University of Miami. She holds a master's degree in education with a specialization in foreign language education. She has seven years' experience teaching Spanish at the secondary level in both traditional and online formats and is bilingual in English and Spanish. Her research focuses on best practices for literacy and language instruction to support English language learners and bilingual learners in the primary school context.

**PETER C. KUNZE** holds a PhD in English from Florida State University and is currently completing a PhD in media studies at the University of Texas at Austin. His research examines the intersection of creativity, culture, and industry, with a special focus on children's media culture. He edited *The Films of Wes Anderson: Critical Essays on an Indiewood Icon* and *Conversations with Maurice Sendak*.

**JOSEY MCDANIEL** recently accepted a position in the Florida Department of Education overseeing principal preparation programs and leadership contracts. She was an eleventh- and twelfth-grade English teacher at Lawton Chiles High School in Tallahassee, Florida. She earned her BS degree in English education and her MS degree in educational leadership from Florida State University. McDaniel is interested in pursuing an EDD in educational technology because she believes the utilization of educational software is the future of innovative instruction. She is interested in educational approaches that incorporate current trends in literacy, social dynamics, and relativism.

**KATIE RYBAKOVA, PhD,** is an assistant professor of education at Thomas College in Maine. She also serves as the executive director for the Maine Association for Middle Level Education. She earned her doctorate from Florida State University in curriculum and instruction. Her research focuses on digital literacies and adolescent literacies.

**JILL SLAY** is a secondary library media specialist (LMS) at Putnam City West High School in Oklahoma City, Oklahoma. Before becoming an LMS, Jill taught AP English literature and AP English language. She also serves as a Fellow for Oklahoma A+ Schools. She has been an educator for seventeen years.

**SHARON L. SMITH** is a doctoral student specializing in literacy and language learning for multilingual students in the Department of Teaching and Learning at the University of Miami. She holds bachelor's degrees in elementary education and Spanish with a specialization in reading instruction from Purdue University. After completing a Fulbright English Teaching Assistant Program grant in Colombia, she taught elementary school for two years before pursuing her PhD. Her research focuses on best practices for literacy and language instruction to support emerging bilingual learners in the elementary school context.

**REBECCA WEBER** is the education and teaching librarian at Oklahoma State University. She was previously an instruction librarian at Florida Institute of Technology. She manages the Mary L. Williams Education and Teaching Library and serves as a liaison to the College of Education, Health and Aviation. One of her primary research interests is the intersection between information literacy and curriculum development.

# INDEX